Leckie×Leckie
Scotland's leading educational publishers

D1391045

5/2010

Practice Papers for SQA Exams

Higher

Business Management

ISBN 978-1-84372-800-9

Published by
Leckie & Leckie Ltd, 4 Queen Street, Edinburgh, EH2 1JE
Tel: 0131 220 6831 Fax: 0131 225 9987
enquiries@leckieandleckie.co.uk www.leckieandleckie.co.uk

A CIP Catalogue record for this book is available from the British Library.

Leckie & Leckie Ltd is a division of Huveaux plc.

Questions and answers in this book do not emanate from SQA. All of our entirely new and original Practice Papers have been written by experienced authors working directly for the publisher.

Leckie & Leckie makes every effort to ensure that all paper used in its books is made from wood pulp obtained from well-managed forests, controlled sources and recycled wood or fibre.

Leckie & Leckie would like to thank the following for permission to reproduce their copyright material without charge:

STV for the STV logo on p. 12
British Airways for the British Airways logo on p. 20

Introduction

Layout of the Book

This book contains practice exam papers, which mirror the actual SQA exam as much as possible. The layout, paper colour and question level are all similar to the actual exam that you will sit, so that you are familiar with what the exam paper will look like.

The answer section is at the back of the book. Each answer gives a solution or a range of solutions to see how the correct answer could be arrived at in order to pick up the marks for the question. The answers also include practical tips on how to tackle certain types of questions, details of how marks are awarded and advice on just what the examiners will be looking for.

Revision advice is provided in this introductory section of the book, so please read on!

How to use This Book

The Practice Papers can be used in two main ways:

1. You can complete an entire practice paper as preparation for the final exam. If you would like to use the book in this way, you can either complete the practice paper under exam style conditions by setting yourself a time for each paper and answering it as well as possible without using any references or notes. Alternatively, you can answer the practice paper questions as a revision exercise, using your notes to produce a model answer. Your teacher or lecturer may mark these for you. Please remember that the examination for Higher Business Management is split into 2 Sections. In Section 1 you have no choice of questions in which to answer. However, in Section 2 of the paper you are required to choose 2 questions to answer from a choice of 5. You need to make sure you read all questions carefully before deciding which 2 to answer; do not start a question and then decide half way through you can not complete it. Once you have finished completing a practice paper under examination conditions, it is important to go back and tackle the remaining 3 questions that you did not originally answer so that you get the best possible benefit from this book.

2. You can use the Topic Index to find all the questions within the book that deal with a specific topic so that you can revise for end of topic tests and your internal assessments. This allows you to focus specifically on areas that you particularly want to revise or, if you are mid-way through your course, it lets you practise answering exam-style questions for just those topics that you have studied.

Revision Advice

Revision for your examinations is essential. Create a revision timetable for each week's work in advance – remember to cover all of your subjects and to leave time for homework and breaks. You will need to change this revision timetable to take account of the examinations you have in a particular week. For example:

Day	6pm–6.45pm	7pm–8pm	8.15pm–9pm	9.15pm–10pm
Monday	Homework	Homework	Business Management Revision	Chemistry Revision
Tuesday	Maths Revision	Accounting Revision	Homework	Free
Wednesday	Geography Revision	Modern Studies Revision	English Revision	French Revision
Thursday	Homework	Maths Revision	Chemistry Revision	Free
Friday	Business Management Revision	French Revision	Free	Free
Saturday	Free	Free	Free	Free
Sunday	Modern Studies Revision	Maths Revision	Accounting Revision	Homework

Make sure that you have at least one evening free a week to relax, socialise and re-charge your batteries. It also gives your brain a chance to process the information that you have been feeding it all week.

Arrange your study time into one hour or 30 minutes sessions, with a break between sessions e.g. 6pm – 7pm, 7.15pm – 7.45pm, 8pm – 9pm. Try to start studying as early as possible in the evening when your brain is still alert and be aware that the longer you put off starting, the harder it will be to start!

Study a different subject in each session, except for the day before an exam.

Do something different during your breaks between study sessions – have a cup of tea, or listen to some music. Don't let your 15 minutes expand into 20 or 25 minutes though!

Have your class notes and any textbooks available for your revision to hand as well as plenty of blank paper, a pen, etc.

Writing in your Examination

Before you start writing an answer to a question, assume that the person reading your answer knows nothing. You should explain each concept clearly and in enough detail but without making it too wordy – keep to the point and question.

In your examination, you should be writing in full sentences (no one-word answers!) and you should try to avoid using bullet points. Using bullet points will make your answer read like a list and in some questions (eg discuss questions) this is a big no!

Knowing and using the correct Business Management terms and words is crucial to your examination success, so you may wish to create a list of the key concepts you come across in your revision. For example:

Key Concepts	Meaning
Retailer	An organisation who distributes products to the customer on behalf of the manufacturer.
Mechanisation	Machinery as well as some degree of labour is used in the production process.
Span of control	The number of subordinates who report to a person.

Transfer Your Knowledge

As well as using your class notes and textbooks to revise, these practice papers will also be a useful revision tool as they will help you to get used to answering exam style questions. You may find as you work through the questions that they refer to a case study or an example that you haven't come across before. Don't worry! You should be able to transfer your knowledge of a topic or theme to a new example. The enhanced answer section at the back will demonstrate how to read and interpret the question to identify the topic being examined and how to apply your course knowledge in order to answer the question successfully.

Leckie & Leckie has published a range of excellent resources for you to use when revising for Higher Business Management: *Intermediate 2 & Higher Business Management Course Notes, 2nd edition, Higher Business Management Success Guide* and *Higher Business Management Grade Booster.*

Command Words

In the practice papers and in the exam itself, a number of command words will be used in the questions. These command words are used to show you how you should answer a question – some words indicate that you should write more than others. If you familiarise yourself with these command words, it will help you to structure your answers more effectively.

Command Word	Meaning/Explanation
Identify	Giving a list is acceptable here – as a general rule you will get one mark for each point you give. However, you won't find many of these types of questions in the Higher Business Management exam!
Outline	Give a brief description or overview of what you are talking about
Describe	Provide a detailed description; give more detail than you would in an outline and use examples where you can.
Explain	Discuss why an action has or might be taken or an outcome reached – what are the reasons and/or processes behind it.
Justify	Give reasons for your answer; you should be making an argument for the suggestion you have given.
Compare	Give the key features of 2 or more different items or ideas and discuss their similarities and/or their differences.
Discuss	Look at an issue closely giving reasons for and against a particular argument.
Distinguish	The differences between 2 or more factors should be highlighted.

In the Exam

Watch your time and pace yourself carefully. Work out roughly how much time you can spend on each answer and try to stick to this.

You must answer all the questions in section one and any 2 questions from section two.

The practice papers will help you to become familiar with the exam's instructions. It is **very** important that you follow the instructions given on the front of the examination paper so make sure you read this carefully. When you begin your actual SQA examination, read the instructions very carefully on the front of the paper and through out the paper in case these have changed.

Read the question thoroughly before you begin to answer it – make sure you know exactly what the question is asking you to do.

Do not repeat yourself in each answer as you will not get any more marks for saying the same thing twice. This also applies to annotated diagrams which will not get you any extra marks if the information is repeated in the written part of your answer. Remember to label any diagrams (eg product life cycle or stock control) carefully and correctly.

Give proper explanations. A common error is to give descriptions rather than explanations. If you are asked to explain something, you should be giving reasons. Check your answer to an 'explain' question and make sure that you have used plenty of linking words and phrases such as 'because', 'this means that', 'therefore', 'so', 'so that', 'due to', 'since' and 'the reason is'.

Exam practice and revision is the key to exam success.

Remember – everyone revises differently, so find a way that works for you!

TOPIC INDEX

Your examination will cover all 3 units (and every topic) in the Higher course:

Unit 1 Business Enterprise
Unit 2 Business Decision Areas: Marketing and Operations
Unit 3 Business Decision Areas: Finance and Human Resource Management

	EXAM A		EXAM B		EXAM C		EXAM D	
	Section 1	Section 2	Section 1	Section 2	Section 1	Section 2	Section 1	Section 2
Unit 1								
Topic – Business in Contemprary Society								
Role of business in society	5							
Types of business organisations	3					1(c)		2(c,i,ii) 4(e)
Business objectives		3(a,i)	1(a,i)		1(b)			
Role of enterprise & the entrepreneur					4(c)			
Stakeholders		5(c)			3(d)			3(e,ii)
Sources of finance		2(b)	1(a,ii) 3(e)					
Sources of assistance								5(d,i,ii)
Growth		4(c,i,ii)		3(a,b)		3(a,b)		
External factors on business	7	3(a,ii)		2		4		
Topic – Business Information and ICT								
Sources of information			2(a,i,ii)		1(c,ii)		3(d)	
Types of information	9				1(c,i)		3(a)	
Value of information		2(c)			4(b)			
Uses of ICT		4(d)	4	5(a,ii)	5(a,i)		1(e)	
ICT legislation		1(c,ii)			3(c)		3(b)	
Topic – Decision making								
Role of management in decision making		1(b,ii)	3(a,b)	3(b,ii)		5(a,ii)		
Types of decisions		1(b,i)		3(b,i)	1(e)		7(a)	
Decision making models & problems				5(d)			7(b)	

	EXAM A		EXAM B		EXAM C		EXAM D	
	Section 1	Section 2	Section 1	Section 2	Section 1	Section 2	Section 1	Section 2
Unit 1								
Topic – Internal Organisation								
Grouping of organisation activities		4(a,i,ii)				2(b,i,ii)	5(b)	
Forms of organisational structure				3(c)				4(d,i,ii)
Corporate culture	5			3(d)				3(c)
Aspects of organisational structure		5(d)		4(d)				
Unit 2								
Topic – Marketing								
The Marketing concept		2(a), 5(b,ii)						2(e)
Product	8			1(b,i,ii)	4	4(a)		
Price			6(a,b)					4(c)
Place & distribution channels						3(a)		1(a,i,ii)
Promotion	4			4(e,i,ii)	7(a,b)	1(d)		5(b,i,ii)
Market segmentation				3(a)			5(a)	
Niche marketing		5(b,i)	5					
Field research		3(b,i)				2(d,ii)		
Desk research						2(d,i)		
Sampling		3(b,ii)				3(b)		
Topic – Operations								
Stock control		1(c)			8(a,b)			2(d)
Quality		3(c)		1(d) 2(c)		1(a) 5(b)		5(a,i,ii)
Distribution & delivery		3(d)					8	
Methods of production				2(b,i,ii)	5			4(a)
Labour payment systems								2(a)

	EXAM A		EXAM B		EXAM C		EXAM D	
	Section 1	Section 2	Section 1	Section 2	Section 1	Section 2	Section 1	Section 2
Unit 3								
Topic – Finance								
Final accounts				2(e)		3(e,ii) 5(c)		
Cash flow				4(b,i,ii)		2(a)	2	
Budgeting				4(a)		3(e,i)		
Ratio analysis		4(b)						1(d)
Topic – Human Resource Management								
Human resource planning		1(a)						1(b,i)
Changing employment patterns				4(c)		4(d,i,ii)		4(b)
Recruitment		5(a)	7(a)	1(c)				
Selection		2(d)	7(b)			5(d)		1(b,ii)
Training				5(c)				
Appraisals		1(d)						5(c)
Motivation	2				6			1(c)
Employee relations & industrial action			2	2(d) 3(b,ii)				3(e,i)
HR legislation	6			5(b)				2(b)

Practice Exam A

Business Management: Higher

Practice Papers
For SQA Exams

**Higher Level
Examination A**

Candidate Instructions

You are allowed 2 hours and 30 minutes to complete this paper.

All questions in Section 1 should be answered and in Section 2 only 2 questions should be answered.

Questions should be read carefully before answering.

A total of 100 marks are available in this examination; each section contributing 50 marks.

Scotland's leading educational publishers

SECTION 1

1 hour 15 minutes should be spent on this Section.

Read the case study and then attempt the questions.

UP AND DOWN TIMES FOR STV

BACKGROUND

 Since 1957, STV has been broadcasting a variety of programmes to a varied audience across Scotland. These include dramas, documentaries, entertainment programmes, news broadcasts and special election broadcasts. Today, it broadcasts to approximately £3.5 million people on a weekly basis in every corner of Scotland. It has seen an increase of 13% in the number of people watching their news programmes in the last 5 years. As well as its TV broadcasting, STV also provides an extensive of web based news services on its website, Stv.tv. STV TV listings can be found there and also information on its many programmes.

STV's headquarters is located across the water from the SECC and Clyde Auditorium at Pacific Quay on the recently redeveloped banks of the River Clyde in Glasgow. Its other neighbours include the Glasgow Science Centre, the Clyde Arc and the Crowne Plaza Hotel.

THE PRESENT

STV broadcasts a varied programme schedule including well known dramas, documentaries, entertainment shows and news programmes to an audience across Scotland. News programmes are broadcasted from studios in Glasgow as well as other locations across Scotland, including Edinburgh, Dundee and Aberdeen. The regional news broadcasts (focusing specifically on the news in a particular area) are very popular with viewers and the number of viewers watching these news programmes continues to grow steadily. The broadcaster regularly opts out of the usual Channel 3 network programme schedule in favour of STV produced programmes such as The Hour, STV is Scotland's most popular peak time TV station.

STV has announced cuts to its peak times programme schedule (those programmes shown in the evening during peak hours) and to the loss of well known programmes such as *The Bill* and *Doc Martin*. As a result, some viewers are opting to view eg *The Bill* through satellite or cable on other channels rather than missing out on these all together! These programmes, amongst others, are expensive for STV to broadcast and as a result, the broadcaster have chosen not to show them. Additionally, tough economic conditions are resulting in less advertising revenue and this is a contributing factor as is the need for STV to respond to the ever changing media landscape. STV's also faced with large fees for broadcasting programmes as well as competition from other broadcasters.

This has come at a bad time for STV who are in dispute with ITV over an unpaid debt and tension between the 2 companies is evident in the media. This dispute has resulted in legal action taken by ITV and by STV, who refute ITV's claim.

In August 2009, STV announced that profits have dropped by 84%. In December 2009, the company was worth just under £18 million.

THE FUTURE

There are now more positive times ahead for STV who has partnered with NetPlay TV to be the provider of the first Scotland based live interactive casino channel on digital terrestrial television. It is also producing programmes with a major focus on Scotland and its heritage some of which are very popular with viewers. The last couple of months have also seen its share price increase. STV has been working hard to simplify its structure and reduce its operating costs.

QUESTIONS

	Marks

The information needed to answer these questions will come from the case study as well as the knowledge you have gained during the course.

ALL questions should be attempted.

1. Using the headings given, identify from the case study the problems that STV has faced. (Solutions to problems should not be given.) — **10**

    • Marketing
    • Finance
    • Human Resources
    • External

2. Describe strategies an organisation such as STV could use to motivate its employees. — **6**

3. STV operates as a Public Limited Company (Plc). Explain the advantages and disadvantages of a Plc. — **6**

4. Many organisations pay to advertise their products on television. Justify using television as a form of advertising.

5. Outline the reasons why organisations such as STV and its employees would benefit from having a strong corporate culture. — **5**

6   All organisations have to adhere to various pieces of legislation. Explain the purpose of: — **3**

    • The Data Protection Act 1998
    • The Equal Pay Act 1970
    • Health and Safety at Work Act 1974

7. Many organisations are facing tough economic conditions at the present time. Explain 5 economic influences on an organisation. — **5**

8. STV has a strong brand identity in Scotland.

    (a) Describe what is meant by a brand. — **2**

    (b) Discuss the benefits of having a strong brand identity. — **5**

9. STV has a website providing a range of information for viewers and other interested stakeholders. Describe 4 types of information that may be found on an organisation's website. — **4**

[End of first section] — **(50)**

SECTION 2

1 hour and 15 minutes should be spent on this Section.

TWO questions should be answered.

| | Marks |

1. (a) All organisations must consider their Human Resource. Describe the benefits of Human Resource Planning. **5**

(b) Decision making takes place at all levels in an organisation. **3**

   (i) Distinguish between strategic and operational decision making. **3**

   (ii) There are external and internal factors that impact upon the ability of an organisation to implement decisions. Describe the internal constraints on a manager's ability to implement decisions. **6**

(c) Organisations must choose carefully where to store their stock. Justify the use of a centralised stock storage area. **3**

(d) Discuss the purpose, costs and benefits of an appraisal system. **5**

(25)

2. (a) Marketing is a core organisational activity, one that attracts a huge financial investment by organisations. Explain why organisations invest heavily in marketing activities. **6**

(b) Finance is required by all organisations and is a resource that must be managed carefully. Describe 5 sources of finance that an organisation could use to expand their operations. **5**

(c) Managers require high quality information to enable them to make decisions. Describe the characteristics of high quality information. **8**

(d) Organisations often use a range of selection methods, including testing, when selecting a new employee. Discuss the value of testing as a method of selection. **6**

(25)

	Marks

3. (*a*) (i) All organisations have objectives that they want to achieve. Describe 3 objectives of an organisation operating in the private sector.

    (ii) Other than economic influences, describe 5 external influences that could impact upon an organisation achieving its objectives.

3

5

(*b*) Organisations use market research to help them gather information about what the customer wants.

    (i) Discuss the value of field research in gathering information.

6

    (ii) Distinguish between random sampling and stratified random sampling in selecting participants to take part in market research.

1

(*c*) Describe ways of ensuring an organisation can provide a product or service that is of a high quality.

7

(*d*) The method of distributing finished goods is a decision that an organisation will need to make. Justify transporting finished goods by road.

3

(25)

4. (*a*) Grouping activities by function is a common method of organisational grouping.

    (i) Discuss the use of functional grouping.

6

    (ii) Describe 2 other forms of organisational grouping.

2

(*b*) Ratio analysis can provide an organisation with a useful indicator into their performance. Explain the problems of only using ratio analysis in assessing an organisations performance.

4

(*c*) Organisations can grow in a number of ways and for different reasons.

    (i) Distinguish between divestment and demerger.

1

    (ii) Describe reasons why an organisation would want to expand abroad.

5

(*d*) Many customers are now choosing to purchase goods online. Explain the benefits to the customer of purchasing products online.

7

(25)

5. (*a*) Describe the purpose and use of the following documents used in the recruitment and selection process:

6

➢ Application form
➢ Job description
➢ Person specification

(*b*) (i) Describe what is meant by niche marketing.

2

    (ii) Distinguish between :

2

• differentiated and undifferentiated marketing
• the marketing mix and the product mix

(*c*) All organisations have stakeholder. Describe the interest and influence that 4 stakeholders could have on an organisation.

8

(*d*) Describe what is meant by delayering and explain the possible benefits of delayering.

7

(25)

[End of question paper]

Practice Exam B

Business Management: Higher

Practice Papers
For SQA Examinations

**Higher Level
Examination B**

Candidate Instructions

You are allowed 2 hours and 30 minutes to complete this paper.

All questions in Section 1 should be answered and in Section 2 only 2 questions should be answered.

Questions should be read carefully before answering.

A total of 100 marks are available in this examination; each section contributing 50 marks.

Scotland's leading educational publishers

SECTION 1

1 hour 15 minutes should be spent on this Section.

Read the case study and then attempt the questions.

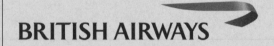

BRITISH AIRWAYS

BACKGROUND

British Airways is a British born company that provides flights to destinations across the world. It is a well established company in the airline industry because it is known and associated with providing a high quality service to its significant number of passengers. Its roots can be traced as far back as 1919 and it has evolved through history as a popular and evolving airline. It was a proud owner of a fleet of Concordes; the only aircraft in the world that could offer supersonic speed flights to parts of the world.

The company flies to hundreds of destinations around the world across all continents. As well flying holidaymakers to international and exotic destinations, it provides a large number of daily services to different airports within the United Kingdom (for example, Aberdeen, Shetland, Edinburgh and Jersey) and Europe (for example, Turkey, Spain, Germany and France). There are considerable numbers of daily flights within the United Kingdom, for example there are currently 4 daily return flights from London Gatwick to Glasgow. These are of course popular with both the business person and holidaymaker who wish to join a connecting flight at a different airport. Many of its flights operate out of London Heathrow and Gatwick Airports, regional airports such as Aberdeen, Inverness and Manchester as well as many smaller airports in remote areas of the country.

People flying on a British Airways flight can enjoy taking advantage of extra services (eg travelling business class) and from the free onboard drink and snack service. This is an uncommon service on 'no frills' airlines and something that British Airways can boast they offer. The company also offers its customers the facility to choose and book their seats before they travel through its website.

JOB LOSSES

Like every other organisation, British Airways relies on its employees to keep it up in the air. Because of a reported loss of £292m for the 6 months to September 2009, it is planning to cut a further 1200 jobs. By Spring 2010 its workforce will have been cut by around 4900 employees. Employees are of course concerned about this and worried about the future of their jobs.

The company is to implement plans to freeze crew pay for 2 years, cut the number of crew on long-haul flights and change the working conditions for new employees.

Employees are unhappy about it and the company are currently in discussions with the Union regarding this but no agreement has yet been reached. There are fears that strike action might be undertaken by cabin crew as a result. Indeed, in December 2009 strike action was planned for over the Christmas season but did not occur because of a ruling by the Courts. In July 2009, the airline's pilots agreed to accept a 2.6% pay cut and some employees have agreed to work part time. Like its Chief Executive in July 2009, some employees (approximately 800) also agreed to work for no financial return in order to help the airline keep costs down.

COST CUTS

British Airways faced a difficult summer in 2009 because of the economic trading conditions. Some people have said that its high ticket prices has not helped because competition low cost airlines on some routes can provide the customer with a cheaper alternative. It has also been reported in the media that it has not responded quickly enough to the changing demands of the customer; customers (particularly business passengers) are seeking low cost fares.

In order to save £22m a year, the company has announced that it will stop offering meals, with the exception of breakfast, which will continue to be offered, on certain short-haul flights. Drinks and snacks will continue to be offered free of charge to passengers, unlike many other airlines. However, there are fears that cutting this service may lose the distinction customers have with the airline compared to budget airlines. However, British Airways does not intend on offering meals for sale on its short-haul flights as other airlines do for an extra cost. Other cost cutting initiatives are also being explored by the airline.

CONCLUSION

Despite the difficult financial situation facing companies like British Airways, it is pleased that its current share price remains strong. What will happen to the company over the next few years remains to be seen.

QUESTIONS

	Marks

The information needed to answer these questions will come from the case study as well as the knowledge you have gained during the course.

ALL questions should be attempted.

1. Using the headings given, identify from the case study the problems that British Airways has faced. (Solutions to problems should not be given.) — **10**

    • Finance
    • Marketing
    • Human Resources
    • External

2. There has been the threat of strike action by British Airways Cabin Crew. Describe 5 other types of industrial action that employees could take. — **5**

3. (a) The management of British Airways have had to make many decisions. Explain the role of management in decision making. — **6**

    (b) Explain how managers would know if their decisions had been effective. — **4**

4. British Airways has a website where customers can purchase tickets and reserve their seats online. Discuss the benefits and costs to a company of having a website. — **6**

5. It could be said that British Airways traditionally operated in a niche market. Describe what is meant by the term niche market. — **2**

6   (a) Describe and justify why organisations use skimming as a pricing strategy. — **4**

    (b) Describe other pricing strategies that could be used by an organisation. — **6**

7. (a) Airlines often use a variety of selection methods including assessment centres when recruiting new employees. Describe and justify the use of an assessment centre. — **4**

    (b) Distinguish between the following human resource terms: — **3**

    • Recruitment and selection
    • Job description and person specification
    • Psychometric test and aptitude test.

[End of first section] — **(50)**

SECTION 2

1 hour and 15 minutes should be spent on this Section.

TWO questions should be answered.

	Marks

1. (a) Local government operates as part of the public sector.

    (i) Describe 2 objectives of local government. — 2

    (ii) Describe 2 sources of finance for a local government. — 2

(b) All products manufactured by an organisation have a life cycle.

    (i) Describe stages of the product life cycle. Use a labelled diagram to support your answer. — 8

    (ii) Explain strategies an organisation could use to extend the life of a product. — 5

(c) Justify why organisations may prefer to recruit internally. — 5

(d) Human Resources is an important aspect in any organisation. Explain how the Human Resources function can contribute to providing a high quality product or service. — 3

(25)

2. (a) All organisations require information to enable them to make decisions.

    (i) Distinguish between primary and secondary information. — 2

    (ii) Explain the benefits of secondary information. — 3

(b) (i) Describe methods of production that an organisation could use. — 3

    (ii) Outline the factors that need to be considered when deciding upon the most suitable method of production. — 2

(c) Organisations can use many methods to ensure quality including the use of quality management. Outline the use of quality management in an organisation. — 5

(d) Explain the impact of poor industrial relations on an organisation. — 4

(e) Organisations prepare various financial statements to aid them in planning and decision making. Outline the information contained in a Trading, Profit & Loss Account. — 6

(25)

	Marks

3. (a) Organisations will often concentrate on providing a product or service to a specific market segment. Describe 5 ways a market could be segmented.

5

(b) Decision making takes places in all organisations at different levels.

   (i) Describe different types of decisions.

3

   (ii) Describe reasons why employees should be encouraged to take part in decision making.

3

(c) Organisations may adopt a matrix structure when people are required to come together to work on a project or a particular task. Discuss the costs and benefits of a matrix structure.

4

(d) Outline the benefits of a strong corporate culture to an organisation.

4

(e) Describe and justify 3 sources of finance that could be used by an organisation when expanding its operations abroad.

6
(25)

4. (a) Explain reasons why organisations might prepare a cash budget.

3

(b) Cash is a very important resource to any organisation and is one that must be managed carefully.

   (i) Explain why a 'just in time' approach to stock management can improve cash flow.

2

   (ii) Describe and justify 3 other methods of improving cash flow.

6

(c) Outline reasons why working practices have changed in the UK over the past 20 years.

4

(d) Relationships between different people and parts of an organisation exist in all organisations. Describe different types of organisational relationships.

3

(e) Organisations may have their products endorsed.

   (i) Describe what is meant by product endorsement.

1

   (ii) Discuss the costs and benefits of product endorsement to an organisation.

6
(25)

5. (a) (i) Organisations may spend large sums of money on technology. Outline reasons why organisations invest heavily in ICT.

5

   (ii) Describe 4 software packages often used by an organisation.

4

(b) Describe reasons why the following pieces of legislation exist:

3

- Computer Misuse Act 1990
- National Minimum Wage Regulations 1999
- Race Relations Act 1976

(c) Training takes place in every organisation and can take many forms. Discuss the use of training in an organisation.

9

(d) When making decisions, organisations may use a structured decision making model in the process. Justify the use of a structured decision making model.

4
(25)

[End of question paper]

Practice Exam C

Business Management: Higher

Practice Papers
For SQA Examinations

**Higher Level
Examination C**

Candidate Instructions

You are allowed 2 hours and 30 minutes to complete this paper.

All questions in Section 1 should be answered and in Section 2 only 2 questions should be answered.

Questions should be read carefully before answering.

A total of 100 marks are available in this examination; each section contributing 50 marks.

Scotland's leading educational publishers

SECTION 1

1 hour 15 minutes should be spent on this Section.

Read the case study and then attempt the questions.

DIAGEO

BACKGROUND

Diageo Plc is a popular manufacturer of a range of alcoholic drinks. It is well known and has a well established brand identity across the globe. Its brands include the famous Baileys (and variety of Baileys flavours), Archers, Smirnoff and Johnnie Walker. The Johnnie Walker brand (an internationally leading scotch whisky) has had particular connections with Kilmarnock in Ayrshire since 1820. The company has a number of operating plants across Scotland including those in Glasgow, Fife and Ayrshire but it is well known for its diverse range of products across the globe. It has a well known place in the international drinks market.

Diageo was formed in 1997 following the merger of 2 companies called Grandmet and Guiness, but its history dates back into the eighteenth and nineteeth centuries. Its name derives from the Latin and Greek dictionaries meaning day (Dia) and world (geo) respectively. As a Public Limited Company, it is managed by a Board of Directors who report to its shareholders. Despite some of the problems it has faced, its share price in 2009 did not weaken. It employs over 22000 people across 80 different countries making it a large international business organisation and employer.

Diageo prides itself in combining a mixture of labour and capital in its production process and at the same time producing an extremely high quality product. It uses a variety of production techniques to ensure it produces a very high quality product in order to retain its strong identity.

Its business strategy, mission statement and vision is based upon 5 core themes: passionate about customers, value each other, freedom to succeed, proud of what we do and be the best. Like many other organisations, Diageo places its customers at the heart of its business activities and realises their importance and indeed its vision reflects this.

RESTRUCTURING

Diageo announced in 2009 that it was to restructure its operations with the loss of up to 900 jobs from the 4000 people employed in its Scottish plants over the next 2 years. These job losses would come from closing a distillery in Port Dundas, Glasgow and from a Kilmarnock packaging plant.

The job cuts at Kilmarnock were as a result of 'infrastructure limitations' but some of the job losses would be offset by job creations elsewhere. Disgruntled and unhappy employees held protests in Kilmarnock and Diageo bosses expressed concerns that they were scared this would have particular consequences for the Johnnie Walker brand and that future investors of the company would be put off from investing.

Weakened world markets and constantly changing turbulent economic conditions had an impact upon the decisions being made, and sales from the January-March 2009 period of trading were down 7%. Reductions in the level of stock being held in the United States were also an issue for the company.

Rising financial costs, together with specific tax increases in some countries (eg 70% increase in Australia) on particular products were undoubtedly hitting upon Diageo's financial position and cash flow. In short, the cost of trading was becoming expensive.

THE FUTURE

Diageo believes that it is in a good position to go forward because of the diverse range of products it has. Despite job cuts in certain locations, it has invested money in creating new jobs in other locations. It is active and entrepreneurial in seeking new business opportunities across the globe and in strengthening its brand identity. It has a commitment to promoting responsible drinking habits and in reducing its impact upon the environment.

QUESTIONS

The information needed to answer these questions will come from the case study as well as the knowledge you have gained during the course.

ALL questions should be attempted.

Marks

1. Using the headings given, identify from the case study the problems that Diageo has faced. (Solutions to problems should not be given.)

   - Finance
   - Human Resources
   - External

   10

2. Diageo along with many other organisations face increasing external pressure on their operations. Explain how 6 external influences could impact upon an organisation.

   6

3. Diageo was formed in 1997 by the merger of Guiness and Grandmet.

   (a) Describe the advantages of a merger.

   4

   (b) Describe forms of integration as a method of growth.

   4

4. Before launching a new product, organisations have a range of activities to carry out. Explain these activities that organisations carry out before launching a new product onto the market.

   5

5. Distinguish between reasons why organisations may use a mixture of capital and labour in its production process.

   4

6. The prospect of job losses at any organisation can cause morale amongst the workforce to suffer. Explain strategies to encourage a productive workforce.

   6

7. (a) Explain the importance of good public relations to an organisation.

   2

   (b) Describe 3 methods an organisation could use to improve its public relations.

   3

8. All organisations must manage their stock and will have systems in place to do this effectively.

   (a) Explain the importance of the 4 stages involved in a stock control management system.

   4

   (b) Justify the use of a computerised stock control management system.

   2

[End of first section]

(50)

SECTION 2

1 hour and 15 minutes should be spent on this Section.

TWO questions should be answered.

		Marks

1. (*a*) Organisations must ensure that they provide a product that is of the highest quality. Explain the factors that contribute towards providing a good quality product. **4**

(*b*) Most businesses have a mission statement. Outline and describe the purpose of a mission statement. **2**

(*c*) (i) Organisations use various types of information in their day to day operations. Describe 5 types of such information. **5**

(ii) Describe what is meant by the source primary information and discuss the value of it to an organisation that an organisation may use. **8**

(*d*) All organisations spend large sums of money on promotional activities. Outline the purpose of promotion activities. **3**

(*e*) Decision making can occur in different places within an organisation. Compare centralised and decentralised decision making. **3**

(25)

2. (*a*) All organisations must manage their cash flow effectively or run the risk of having a poor cash flow. Describe reasons why an organisation may have a poor cash flow. **5**

(*b*) (i) Outline methods that could be used by an organisation to organise their activities. **5**

(ii) Explain the factors that will impact upon which activity grouping an organisation will choose. **4**

(*c*) A public corporation is a type of business organisation. Describe the ownership and control of a public corporation. **2**

(*d*) (i) All organisations carry out research to find out what their customers want. Justify why organisations carry out desk research in this process. **3**

(ii) Outline the use of observations as a method of market research. **6**

(25)

			Marks

3. (a) Organisations can choose which distribution channels to source their products from. Explain the benefits to a retailer of sourcing products from a wholesaler.

3

(b) When carrying out market research, it would be impossible to ask every member of the population to participate and it is for this reason that sampling is used. Describe 3 methods of sampling.

3

(c) Outline the purpose and principles of the Data Protection Act.

6

(d) Describe the interest and influence of the local community on an organisation.

6

(e) (i) Explain the benefits of preparing a cash budget.

4

    (ii) Describe what is meant by the following financial terms:

3

- Liquidity
- Trade Credit
- Fixed Assets

(25)

4. (a) Discuss the advantages and disadvantages to an organisation of having a well established brand identity.

9

(b) High quality information is essential in the successful running of a business organisation. Describe the qualities associated with high quality information.

7

(c) Describe the role and characteristics associated with an entrepreneur.

4

(d) (i) Distinguish between the following flexible working practices:

2

- Homeworking and teleworking
- Temporary and fixed term contracts

    (ii) Justify why organisations should adopt flexible working practices.

3

(25)

5. (a) (i) ICT can be used by organisations for a range of reasons including decision making. Explain the benefits of using ICT in decision making.

6

    (ii) Decision making occurs at all levels of an organisation. Describe the factors an organisation would consider when deciding if a decision they had made had been done effectively.

4

(b) All organisations must provide a high quality product to their customers. Describe ways companies such can ensure that they provide a high quality product.

8

(c) Outline the information that will be found in an organisation's balance sheet.

4

(d) Many organisations ask applicants to complete an application form when applying for a job vacancy. Justify why they do this.

3

(25)

[End of question paper]

Practice Exam D

Business Management: Higher

Practice Papers
For SQA Exams

**Higher Level
Examination D**

Candidate Instructions

You are allowed 2 hours and 30 minutes to complete this paper.

All questions in Section 1 should be answered and in Section 2 only 2 questions should be answered.

Questions should be read carefully before answering.

A total of 100 marks are available in this examination; each section contributing 50 marks.

Leckie × Leckie
Scotland's leading educational publishers

SECTION 1

1 hour 15 minutes should be spent on this Section.

Read the case study and then attempt the questions.

HOME OR AWAY?

BACKGROUND

Everyone enjoys a nice holiday; whether it involves lying on a golden sand beach in Spain, viewing the sites, building and attractions in New York or camping in the Highlands of Scotland. People enjoy being able to get away from the stress, strains and demands of everyday life and to be able to relax, unwind, and enjoy the weather and sites that their chosen holiday destination has to offer. Of course, it's not just the lucky holidaymakers who benefit from this, but also the tour operators and airlines that offer these holidays. Tour operators and airlines are fortunate in being able to offer a service that so many people see as an essential part of life; indeed, we are constantly reminded of this through lots of advertising on television, the internet and through shops up and down our High Streets. You don't have to walk far down a street in a town centre or shopping centre to find a tour operator or airline's shop in front of you, boasting about the deals that packages it has to offer.

FOGGY FUTURE

However, not all is sunny and hot for our tour operators and their future is somewhat foggy and cold. Business analysts have forecasted however that tour operators should be concerned about their future for a number of reasons. The economic downturn and rising unemployment has forced consumers to tighten the strings on their purses and as a result, demand for the services offered by tour operators is down; people can simply not afford to pay for a trip and instead are choosing to either not go on a foreign holiday, or instead to stay and take advantage of what their own country has to offer. Tour operators are facing increasing operating costs, including the high duty to be paid on fuel because of high oil prices. Rising costs are a concern to all companies, because higher costs means lower profits (or ultimately a larger loss).

Early in 2009, further problems awaited the airline industry when the outbreak of swine flu originating from Mexico, forced the tour operators to reschedule flights and refund customers. They did this as a precaution to help stop the spread of swine flu from Mexico into the United Kingdom. The restrictions did not last too long, and after a short time flights were operating as planned and people taking their no doubt well deserved holiday.

Thomas Cook and Thomson's, two large tour operators are feeling the pressure placed upon them and their share price has fallen. They each offer the holiday maker a large choice of destinations across the globe and a number of luxury and exotic trips. No frills airline, Easyjet has seen its profits dip by 65% and it is  concerned about a tough winter ahead. More recently, some airlines are concerned about the proposed merger of British Airways and Spain's Iberia and in December 2009, Globespan (a Scottish-based holiday and airline company) went into administration. It had offered its customers a range of packages to suit all purses to a number of popular destinations, including Florida, Canada and other European destinations.

STAY AT HOME?

However, not everybody chooses to take a foreign holiday and many people decided to stay at home in 2009 rather than taking a trip abroad and why not? Scotland has a fantastic range of tourist attractions up and down its coast to be taken advantage of and if you can't have the sunny beaches of Tenerife or the heat of the desert, why not settle for a nice walk down the Scottish coast?

QUESTIONS

	Marks

The information needed to answer these questions will come from the case study as well as the knowledge you have gained during the course.

ALL questions should be attempted.

1. Using the headings given, identify from the case study the problems that holiday operators have faced. (Solutions to problems should not be given.)   **10**

    • Finance
    • Marketing
    • External

2. Cash flow problems are a concern for the airline industry. Describe 6 reasons why cash flow problems may occur.   **6**

3. (a) It has been proposed that British Airways and Iberia merge. Describe what is meant by the term merger.   **1**

    (b) Explain 3 advantages of a merger to the organisations that are merging.   **3**

4. External influences impact upon all business organisations. Explain how 6 different external influences could impact upon the running of a company.   **6**

5. (a) Many holiday companies target their products towards particular market segments. Describe 5 different segments that companies could gear their product towards.   **5**

    (b) Holiday companies may group their activities according to the specific type of customer. Describe 4 other types of activity grouping.   **4**

6. (a) One example of a decision that holiday companies had to make was whether or not to offer services to Mexico when the swine flu broke out. Describe different types of decisions that organisations make.   **6**

    (b) Decision making can be a complex process and some organisations use structured-decision making models to help in the process. Justify the use of such models.   **5**

7. Some people think aircrafts are only used to transport passengers. However, the use of airlines to transport products is not uncommon. Discuss the use of air to transport products.   **4**

   (50)

[End of first section]

SECTION 2

1 hour and 15 minutes should be spent on this Section.

TWO questions should be answered.

	Marks

1. (a) (i) Outline 4 channels of distribution that could be used by an organisation. **4**

      (ii) Describe the factors that restrict the choice of a channel of distribution. **4**

  (b) (i) The Human Resource function in any organisation provides a crucial role in the successful achievement of an organisation's aims. Outline the role of the Human Resource function. **5**

      (ii) One of the tasks an HR Department would be involved in is carrying out interviews. Compare a one-to-one interview with a panel interview. **3**

  (c) Describe methods that an organisation could adopt to encourage their employees to work as hard as possible. **5**

  (d) Distinguish between the following accounting ratios: **2**

     • Gross Profit Percentage and Net Profit Percentage
     • Current (Working Capital) and Acid Test (Quick)

  (e) Explain the advantages of e-mail to communicate with other people. **2**

(25)

2. (a) Organisations can pay their employees using a variety of methods. Compare different payment systems that could be used by organisations to pay their employees. **3**

  (b) Describe the purpose of the following pieces of legislation: **4**

     • Sex Discrimination Act
     • Data Protection Act
     • Health and Safety at Work Act
     • Equal Pay Act

  (c) (i) Many fast food chains operate as a franchise. Describe the term franchise. **2**

      (ii) Explain the advantages and disadvantages of franchising to the franchisor. **5**

  (d) Justify the use of a high-quality and reliable supplier of raw materials. **3**

  (e) Marketing is often referred to as a strategic activity and an important part of an organisation's operations. Justify the importance of each element of the marketing mix. **8**

(25)

	Marks

3. (*a*) Many organisations have a website that can be used by customers to make purchases. Describe 4 types of information that may be found on an organisation's website. — **4**

(*b*) Describe the purpose and principles of the Computer Misuse Act 1990. — **4**

(*c*) Describe the benefits to an organisation of having a strong corporate culture. — **5**

(*d*) Distinguish between primary and secondary information. — **3**

(*e*) All organisations have stakeholders who have an interest in its activities and who can influence it in a number of ways.

  (i) Explain how the employees of an organisation can influence its behaviour. — **3**

  (ii) Describe the interest of 3 external stakeholders in an organisation. — **6**

(25)

4. (*a*) Describe the methods of producing different types of products. — **3**

(*b*) Explain the reasons why there has been a decline in manufacturing in the United Kingdom over the past 20 years. — **3**

(*c*) Pricing is a very important element of the marketing mix. Distinguish between 4 pricing strategies that could be used by an organisation. — **4**

(*d*) (i) Explain what is meant by an entrepreneurial structure. — **1**

  (ii) Discuss the benefits of an entrepreneurial structure. — **4**

(*e*) (i) Discuss the structure and features of the public sector in terms of ownership and control. — **6**

  (ii) Describe 4 objectives a public sector organisation could have. — **4**

(25)

				Marks

5. (*a*) (i) Explain what is meant by the following terms:

      • Benchmarking
      • Quality assurance
      • Quality circles

    3

    (ii) Suggest reasons why organisations spend a significant amount of resources on ensuring they have quality inputs.

    4

(*b*) (i) Promotion activities can consist of advertising, promotions and celebrity endorsement. Explain the advantages and disadvantages of product endorsement.

    4

    (ii) Describe reasons why the Advertising Standards Authority exists and describe the influence it can have on organisations.

    3

(*c*) Describe the advantages and disadvantages of an appraisal.

    6

(*d*) (i) Starting up a new business is not always a straight forward task. Identify places where a new entrepreneur may find help with starting a new business.

    2

    (ii) Outline the types of information the new entrepreneur may obtain from the places identified in d(i).

    3

    (25)

[End of question paper]

Worked Answers

SECTION 1

1. **Marketing**
   - Tough economic conditions.
   - Changing media landscape.
   - Competition from other broadcasters.
   - Less advertising revenue.

   Finance
   - Profits drop 84%.
   - ITV chasing an unpaid debt.
   - Expensive charges for programmes.
   - Less advertising revenue.

   Human Resources
   - Feared job losses in Glasgow and in other locations such as Aberdeen and Dundee.
   - Employee morale has been affected.

   External
   - Tough economic conditions.
   - Changing media landscape.
   - Ongoing tension and dispute between STV and ITV.
   - Legal action is being taken by ITV.

   1 mark per correctly identified problem.
   Maximum of 3 marks per heading
   (10 marks maximum for question).

> **TOP EXAM TIP**
>
> Write down the headings given in the question (eg Marketing) and write down the problems you have identified from the case study under the appropriate heading.

2. **Any 6 from:**

   Financial incentives (eg bonuses for meeting sales targets) could be provided as a way of encouraging employees to work hard and meet targets. (1 mark)

   Social activities that involve members of the organisation coming together could be arranged. (1 mark)

   Allowing employees to take advantage of flexible working practices such as homeworking (1 mark) can motivate employees as it allows them to manage their work/life balance and juggle their work and personal commitments to suit their needs. (1 mark)

   Providing training to employees so that they can improve their skills and performance at work. (1 mark)

   Encourage employee to participate in Quality Circles and/or Works Councils so that they can express their views on matters impacting upon them. (1 mark)

   Profit sharing schemes whereby employees share part of the organisation's profit.(1 mark)

Employees should be given regular positive feedback on their performance and where necessary improvements that need to be made for example through an appraisal system. (1 mark)

Employees could be given the opportunity to try out new jobs and widen their skills (or introducing job rotation whereby employees get to undertake a variety of different tasks). (1 mark)

> **HINT** This question encourages you to think about the course as a whole and how some of the different topics you have studied can be also be strategies to motivate employees. You won't always find a section in your textbook or notes on 'Motivating Employees'!

3. **Advantages**

   Shareholders benefit from limited liability – this means they will only lose the money invested in the company if the company was to go bankrupt and therefore the responsibility and risk is shared (1 mark)

   The organisation can benefit from the range of experiences and skills that shareholders and Directors bring. (1 mark)

   Plcs can obtain more sources of finance compared to some other types of business organisations eg Debentures. (1 mark)

   Disadvantages

   It is more complicated to set up a Plc compared to eg a sole trader or partnership because there are legal requirements to be complied with and documents (eg Memorandum and Articles of Association) to be prepared. (1 mark)

   Once set up, the company is bound by the rules and regulations provided in the Companies Act whereas other types of organisations such as a sole trader or partnership do not have this. (1 mark)

   A Plc must publicly publish its annual final accounts and these would be available for competitors to see. (1 mark)

> **HINT** You must explain advantages and disadvantages in your answer because the question has asked for these.

4. Advertising on television has many benefits. Large audiences watch television and therefore will see the advert being shown. (1 mark)

   Advertisements can be shown during specific types of programmes so that the intended market segment is targeted. (1 mark)

   Unlike advertising in some newspapers, products can be shown on television in colour. (1 mark)

   The product being advertised can be shown from different angles and demonstrations of the product in action can be shown. (1 mark)

5. The benefits of a strong corporate culture are:

   Employees feel they belong and are part of the organisation. (1 mark)

   Efficiency and productivity for the organisation can increase. (1 mark)

   Positive relationships can be created and maintained which helps improve employee relations. (1 mark)

Employee loyalty can be increased (1 mark)

Image and identity of the organisation can be improved. (1 mark)

> **HINT** Only the *benefits* of a strong corporate culture are required.

6. The purpose of the Data Protection Act is to control the way organisations collect, store, process and distribute information. This is to protect both individuals and other organisations. (1 mark)

    The purpose of the Equal Pay Act 1970 is to ensure that both men and women receive the same rate of pay for doing work considered of equal value. (1 mark)

    The purpose of the Health and Safety at Work Act 1974 is to ensure the health and safety of everyone in the workplace. It details the responsibilities of both the employer and employee to ensure the health and safety of everyone in the workplace. (1 mark)

7. Interest rates means that the cost of borrowing (eg taking out a bank loan) could be expensive if the rate is high. (1 mark)

    Exchange rates can make it expensive to trade with countries who use a different currency because the value of the pound would be low. (1 mark)

    High levels of inflation cause the cost of purchasing goods (eg raw materials) to be high and therefore costs are higher. (1 mark)

    A recession means that demand would decrease and the organisation would suffer from less sales as a result of less people spending their money. (1 mark)

    A boom period means that demand would increase and the organisation would benefit from more sales being made which in turn will increase their sales revenue. (1 mark)

> **HINT** To gain each mark in this question, you must say how each economic influence would impact upon the organisation. (This is because it is an **explain** question).

8. (a) A brand is the term given to a name, symbol or logo that identifies a product or organisation. (1 mark)

    A brand is used to distinguish between similar products offered by competitors. (1 mark)

> **HINT** As there are 2 marks for a description of a brand, you need to make sure you make at least 2 separate points.

    (b) A strong brand allows the organisation and/or its products to be easily recognised. (1 mark) Strong brand names are often associated with a good quality product (1 mark) which in turn can lead to an increased loyalty to be established between the organisation and its customers. (1 mark) In addition, because a strong brand is often associated with high quality, the organisation can command a higher price for its product. (1 mark) Finally, when the organisation is attempting to introduce new products to the market a strong brand identity means that they can often do this much more successfully compared to an organisation without it. (1 mark)

9. Any 4 for one mark each:

Written – is written down using text eg letters, memos, reports, newspaper articles.
Oral/Verbal – is spoken and then heard eg discussions, interviews, presentations.
Pictorial – this is information presented through pictures or photos
Graphical – this is information presented through a chart or graph.
Numerical – information presented through numbers eg on a spreadsheet.
Quantitative – this information is factual and can be counted or measured.
Qualitative – this information includes opinions, views and judgements.

SECTION 2

1. (a) Human resource (HR) planning contributes to achieving organisational objectives. (1 mark) It is essential in keeping up to date with changing patterns of employment and in enabling organisations to take action if changes to staffing levels, contracts and working practices are required. (1 mark) The skills required for future jobs in the organisation is considered as part of HR planning and this will ensure that the organisation has the necessary skilled people to do these jobs. (1 mark) If necessary, training programmes to meet requirements of changing job requirements can be arranged. (1 mark) Without HR planning, organisations could waste money on unnecessary or ineffective resources but HR planning should avoid this. (1 mark)

> **TOP EXAM TIP**
> Knowing what each command word means is crucial in being able to answer questions correctly and pick up the marks.

> **TOP EXAM TIP**
> Notice that bullet points are never used in any answer.

(b) (i) Strategic decisions are concerned with the long-term focus and direction of the organisation whereas operational decisions are ones that impact upon the day to day running of the organisation for a short period of time. (1 mark)

Strategic decisions are made by the Senior Management of a company whereas operational decisions are made by low level managers. (1 mark)

An example of a strategic decision would be whether or not to expand into an overseas market whereas an operational decision could be how many hours to get an employee to work next week. (1 mark)

> **TOP EXAM TIP**
> Distinguish questions require you to think about the difference and not the similarities between 2 or more factors.

(ii) Many factors within an organisation can impact upon a manager's ability to implement decisions for example:

The knowledge, experience and ability of the organisation's staff could prevent a decision being fully implemented. (1 mark)

The financial resource available and that required for successful implementation of the decision could be different. (1 mark)

If staff disagree or do not fully support the decision being implemented this would prevent its successful implementation. (1 mark)

The policy and procedures of the organisation could hinder the speed at which a decision could be implemented. (1 mark)

The time available to implement a decision properly might be shorter than that available. (1 mark)

The quantity and quality of the technology available to implement the decision may not be adequate for the purpose of implementing a decision. (1 mark)

HINT

The question specifically asked for the internal constraints on a manager's ability to **implement** decisions and not simply the internal constraints on making decisions. Your answer needs to be worded in such a way to communicate to the Examiner that you have thought about this (hence why the word 'implemented' appears in each of the descriptions above).

(c) Organisations can monitor the security of stock much more easily when it is stored in only in one place. (1 mark)

It is easier to ensure procedures for receiving, issuing and distributing stock are being implemented and followed across the entire organisation. (1 mark)

TOP EXAM TIP

To justify means to give reasons to support a suggestion or conclusion.

Only storage space in one location is required and this space can be adapted more effectively to suit the stock being held. (1 mark)

(d) An appraisal system aims to ensure employees are working to the best possible standard with the goal of achieving the aims of the organisation. (1 mark) It allows for the strengths and the development needs of an employee to be identified (1 mark) and for the employee to receive feedback from their line manager on their performance at work. (1 mark) Employees who are working extremely well have the opportunity to be identified for promotion (1 mark) and their motivation can increase (1 mark) but those who receive a less positive appraisal can lose the motivation to work hard. (1 mark) Despite it being a time consuming process for an organisation to carry out (1 mark) opportunities for the employee to receive training for the benefit of the organisation can be identified. (1 mark)

HINT

The purpose (or aim) of an appraisal system has been discussed first and then the costs and benefits of an appraisal system are given. The text reads well and all points follow on naturally from each other.

TOP EXAM TIP

Notice that one word answers are never given.

2. (a) Organisations invest heavily in their marketing activities to help them achieve their overall objectives eg in achieving sales maximisation. (1 mark) Marketing activities reminds the customer that the product is still available for them to purchase. (1 mark) They raise awareness of the variety and range of products that the organisation has to offer (1 mark) and provides information about the product to the customer to enable them to make a decision about what to purchase. (1 mark) Certain marketing activities (eg market research) enable an organisation to keep abreast of changing

consumer trends and tastes which can help the organisation predict and then provide the customer with what they want. (1 mark) Finally, organisations can attempt to target and then enter new markets and increase their market share. (1 mark)

> **HINT** This question gets you thinking about the importance and role of marketing.

(b) **Any 5 from:**

Government Grant – A government grant would provide the organisation with money that does not need to be repaid. (1 mark)

Bank Loan – A bank loan must be paid back over a period of time with interest. (1 mark)

Retained Profits – Profits retained from previous years could be invested back into the organisation. (1 mark)

Selling Assets – Assets could be sold (eg property or land) to raise additional finance. (1 mark)

Debentures – Used by Plcs, these are loans obtained from other people or other organisations. Fixed interest is paid to the lender over the loan period and the loan amount is paid back at the end of the agreement. (1 mark)

Venture Capital – usually large loans given to organisations in return for a fee and often for part-ownership of the organisation. (1 mark)

> **HINT** You must be careful in questions that ask you for sources of finance for specific types of organisations. Sole traders or partnerships for example could not raise extra finance through debentures.

(c) Information must be timely – this means that it is available when it is needed and is the most up-to-date information available. (1 mark)

It must be accurate which means that it is error free. (1 mark)

It must be appropriate which means suitable and relevant to the decision being made or task being carried out. (1 mark)

It must be objective which means it is bias free. (1 mark)

It must be concise – brief, straight to the point and free from 'waffle' (1 mark) but at the same time sufficient, meaning there is enough of it to make the decision. (1 mark)

It must be available – it should be obtained as easily as possible. (1 mark)

It must be cost effective – the cost of obtaining the information should be less than the value that it will be provide. (1 mark)

(d) Testing can provide further information about a candidate than was given on a CV or application form or gathered during an interview. (1 mark)

Various types of tests can be carried out depending on the information required and the results of these can be used to assess the applicant's suitability for the job vacancy. (1 mark)

They can be used to prove that the applicant has any necessary skills required for the post (1 mark) and personality tests could be used to determine whether or not the applicant would be suited to the organisation's culture. (1 mark)

However, carrying out tests is a time consuming process for the organisation (1 mark) and an expensive one. (1 mark)

HINT In this question, the answer provides points for and against testing as a method of selection and this is essential in a discuss question to be able to achieve full marks. However, you you do not need to provide the **same amount** of points for and against to be able to obtain full marks.

TOP EXAM TIP

Your answer to a discuss question must contain points for and against, you do not however need to provide an equal number of points for and against.

3. (*a*) (i) **Any 3 from:**

To grow – an organisation may have the aim of growth – this means expanding the organisation into new markets or into new countries. (1 mark)

Become market leader – this means to control and dominate the market within which the organisation operates. (1 mark)

Profit maximisation – to achieve the highest level of profit possible.

Sales maximisation – to generate as much income from sales as possible. (1 mark)

Survival – to exist and continue in business. (1 mark)

To provide a service – to support or help those in need through the provision of a service. (1 mark)

To be socially responsible – for the organisation to be seen to act and behave in a responsible and ethical way. (1 mark)

HINT Remember different types of organisations will have different aims.

(ii) Political influences such as new UK or international laws can prevent or restrict an organisation from doing what they would like. (1 mark)

Social influences such as changing cultures, trends and fashions make it difficult for organisations to predict what customers want. (1 mark)

Technological influences, for example new technology, make it difficult for organisations to keep up-to-date with technological advancements. (1 mark)

Environmental influences – unpredictable weather can impact upon the activities that organisations carry out. (1 mark)

Competition – an increase in competition from home and overseas can impact upon the decisions an organisation makes as well as its customer base. (1 mark)

HINT Any question that asks about external factors should immediately have you thinking 'PESTEC'. This acronym is the easiest way to remember what the external factors on business are: Political, Economic, Social, Technological, Environmental and Competition.

(b) (i) Unlike desk research, field research involves an organisation themselves gathering information for a specific purpose. (1 mark) Information is therefore new and timely. (1 mark) Because they have collected it themselves, the value of the information gathered is going to be higher. (1 mark) Field research may involve carrying out surveys, observations or hall tests and these are costly to carry out (1 mark) and time consuming to conduct (1 mark). The organisation will also require to train individuals in carrying out eg surveys or pay for a specialist market research company to do it for them. (1 mark)

(ii) Random sampling involves simply randomly selecting people from eg the telephone book and then contacting them to participate in the research whereas stratified random sampling involves conducting research with those people based on segments of how the population has been divided. (1 mark)

TOP EXAM TIP

You need to provide both parts to be able to obtain one mark.

(c) In order to produce a quality product or service, organisations needs to ensure that the inputs to the production process such as raw materials, employees and the equipment to be used are of a high quality. (1 mark)

The use of highly skilled, qualified and trained staff who are appropriately supervised is also important. (1 mark)

Quality assurance requires products to be checked at various stages during production. (1 mark)

Quality Management involves the whole organisation (including the workforce) where commitment to quality is second nature. (1 mark)

Quality control involves checking products at the end of the manufacturing process. (1 mark)

Benchmarking involves comparing the organisation's product with the best they can find in the market in an attempt to match standards. (1 mark)

Clearly defined processes or policies should be in place so that everyone knows that is expected and have a standardised process to follow. (1 mark)

Products that meet certain standards can be given quality standards/approval and this communicates to the customer that the product has met specific industry standards. (1 mark)

HINT Questions similar to this are popular in the final examination.

(d) Transporting goods by road is relatively inexpensive compared to other methods. (1 mark)

Goods can be collected at the factory where they are manufactured and delivered directly to the door of the customer. (1 mark)

Products transported by road will not have faced the same conditions or have been handled in the same way as those that have travelled by air (eg extreme temperatures). (1 mark)

4. (*a*) (i) Functional grouping means grouping by functional area or department eg Marketing, Human Resources, Operations, Finance, Research and Development, and is a common method of grouping (1 mark) This grouping provides a structure to the organisation that is clear (1 mark) This grouping allows each department to specialise and concentrate on their own activities. (1 mark) Employees are able to easily consult and seek support from their colleagues from within their department when necessary. (1 mark)

However, this type of structure can cause organisations to be less responsive to changing market conditions. (1 mark) Individual departments can become wrapped in pursuing their own objectives that they lose sight of the organisation's objectives. (1 mark)

(ii) Other methods of organisational grouping include:

Grouping by product or service. This is when activities are grouped based upon the products that the organisation sells. (1 mark)

Geographical grouping (also known as territory grouping). This involves grouping activities based on particular geographical locations. (1 mark)

Customer grouping – grouping by type of customer (1 mark)

Technology grouping – used by manufacturing companies to group activities according to the production process used. (1 mark)

(*b*) The results of ratio analysis is immediately historical and does not consider what may happen in the future. (1 mark) Influences outwith the organisation's control are not considered (eg changes in law, competitors actions, social factors) when carrying out ratio analysis. (1 mark) It is difficult for an organisation to compare and make valid conclusions when they compare their ratios with that of other organisations unless they are of the same size or type. (1 mark) Problems with the workforce such as poor morale or a high level of staff turnover is not considered and this could have impacted upon the results of ratio analysis. (1 mark)

HINT The question only asks for the **problems** and not the **benefits** of using ratio analysis to assess an organisations performance.

(*c*) (i) A demerger is when one organisation splits into 2 separate organisations and divestment is when a organisations sells some of its assets or part of its company to another organisation. (1 mark)

(ii) An organisation may want to expand abroad to take advantage of labour that is available cheaper. (1 mark)

Grants may be available to organisations who choose to set up in particular locations. (1 mark)

By expanding abroad, it could achieve an aim of increasing market share. (1 mark)

An organisation may find it cheaper to expand abroad so that it is closer to its customers rather than having to transport them long distances. (1 mark)

Organisations may expand abroad to move away from competition that may exist in countries that it currently operates in. (1 mark)

HINT — Remember – the question has asked for the reasons why organisations would want to expand abroad, and not the problems (eg language barriers) associated with expanding abroad.

(d) As the internet can be accessed at any time of the day, customers can access information about the organisation and its products as a time that suits them. (1 mark) Organisations often give discounts to customers who purchase online because the organisation does not to employ as many members of staff to assist the customer when making a purchase. (1 mark) Customers who may be some distance from the location of the organisation do not have to travel make a purchase and can do so from the comfort of their own home. (1 mark) Customers are able to make payments online without the need to handle cash with the knowledge that their payment is secure (1 mark) Products can be easily compared online and this enables the customer to make a purchase knowing they are getting the best deal. (1 mark) The availability of products can be checked easily and this allows the customer to quickly source an alternative supplier if the product they wish to purchase is not available. (1 mark) Finally, products can be delivered to the customer's own home without the need for them to travel. (1 mark)

HINT — More than just the advantage of purchasing online needs to be given because this is an **explain** question. A reason why each is an advantage is given and this is essential to be awarded each mark.

5. (a) An application form is prepared by an organisation and is sent to those who are interested in applying for a job vacancy. (1 mark) Applicants are required to answer questions on the application form that will be used by the organisation to assess their suitability for the post applied for. (1 mark)

The purpose of a job description is to communicate information about the job eg role, responsibilities and duties and what it entails. (1 mark) It can be used by the applicant to determine if they had the ability to do the tasks assigned and whether or not they would enjoy and want to do the job. (1 mark)

The purpose of a person specification is to communicate information about the type of person (eg skills, qualities and experience) required to do the job. (1 mark) It can be used by both the applicant and the organisation to assess an individual's suitability for the post applied for eg do they have the necessary skills required for the job. (1 mark)

HINT — In this question you had to think about 2 things: the purpose and use of the documents given. You must ensure that your answer does this to be awarded marks.

(b) (i) Niche marketing – satisfying the needs of specific consumers from a gap identified in the market (1 mark) It involves providing a specialised product that has limited demand and little competition. (1 mark)

(ii) Differentiated marketing focuses on marketing products towards a particular target market whereas undifferentiated marketing focuses on marketing products towards the whole population. (1 mark)

The marketing mix refers to the 4 P's of marketing (product, price, place and promotion) whereas the product mix refers to the range of products that an organisation offers. (1 mark)

(c) **Any 4 from:**

Managers are interested in receiving bonuses and other benefits for their work. (1 mark) They can influence an organisation by making decisions such as what to produce and how much to charge. (1 mark)

Employees want high wages and good working conditions for their work. (1 mark) They can influence an organisation by taking industrial action if they are unhappy with their working conditions. (1 mark)

Customers want high quality products for fair prices. (1 mark) They can influence an organisation by stopping to purchase their products from them and doing so from a competitor. (1 mark)

Suppliers want to be paid on time for the goods they have supplied. (1 mark) They can influence an organisation by changing the amount of money charged for their products. (1 mark)

The Government is interested in receiving money from taxation. (1 mark) They can influence an organisation by changing existing legislation or by introducing new pieces of legislation. (1 mark)

HINT > This type of question is common. Note that you are asked for the **interest** and **influence** of each stakeholder. Your answer must address both of these to gain the marks. Your answer should make it clear why they are interested in an organisation and what they can do to influence it – as the sample answer above does. Remember – competitors are not stakeholders.

(d) Delayering refers to removing levels of management in an organisation structure (1 mark) and is associated with widening the span of control (1 mark). Delayering allows for quicker communication and quicker decision making because there are less levels of authority for communication and instructions to travel though. (1 mark) Because of this, organisations can adapt and take action more quickly to changing market conditions. (1 mark) As managers have a wider span of control, employees often become empowered to make their own decisions and use their own initiative which in turn can increase their motivation and productivity. (1 mark) Delayering will allow the organisation to save money on the salaries of managers because less are required as they have a wider span of control. (1 mark) The managers of the organisation can often feel they have more power because there are fewer of them and they are in charge of more people, this can be motivating to them. (1 mark)

HINT > A **description** of delayering is given, as well as an **explanation** of the benefits it brings.

SECTION 1

1. **Finance**
   - Loss of £292m from March – September 2009.
   - High ticket prices put customers off.

   Marketing
   - High ticket prices put customers off.
   - Increasing competition from low cost airlines.
   - Cheaper flights from other airlines.
   - Changing customer demand.
   - Lack of differentiation between airlines because meal service on short-flights cut.
   - BA not charging for meals – lost revenue.

   Human Resources
   - Job cuts.
   - No agreement with union yet been reached.
   - Unhappy/worried employees because of changing conditions/pay.
   - Threat of strike action by cabin crew.

   External
   - Cheaper tickets being offered by other airlines.
   - Difficult economic trading conditions.
   - Changing customer demand.
   - Competition – cheaper flights from other airlines.

   1 mark per correctly identified problem.
   Maximum of 3 marks per heading.
   (10 marks maximum for question)

   > **HINT** Remember, you must write down the problems under the headings.

2. Five other methods of industrial action (1 mark each):
   Sit in – employees refuse to work and simply sit in the workplace
   Work to rule – only activities written in the contract of employment will be carried out
   Boycott – refusal to carry out a new duty or use a new piece of equipment
   Overtime ban – a refusal to work any time over their normal working hours
   Go slow – employees deliberately work slower than normal

   > **HINT** No marks are given for simply identifying the types of industrial action eg sit in or work-to-rule.

   > **HINT** Remember, the question has asked for other types of industrial action so therefore you would not be given a mark for describing what is meant by a strike.

3. (a) **Any 6 from:**

Plan – to ensure the future needs of the organisation is met so that objectives can be achieved. (1 mark)

Organise – resources need to be available so that tasks can be carried out and decisions implemented effectively. (1 mark)

Command – to ensure tasks are carried out in the manner expected so that they are done to the best possible standard. (1 mark)

Coordinate – necessary resources need to be in the correct place at the correct time so that tasks can be carried out when required. (1 mark)

Control – managers need to ensure tasks are carried out according to the way intended so that decisions and objectives are achieved. (1 mark)

Delegate – some tasks and activities need to be carried out by other people so that managers can concentrate on other work. (1 mark)

Motivate – managers need to motivate their employees so that tasks are carried out to a high standard, on time and in the best possible way. (1 mark)

> **TOP EXAM TIP**
>
> Descriptions need detail – not just the basics.

> *HINT*   No marks are given for identifying the role.

(b) They could look at their financial records to see if sales and profits figures had increased. (1 mark)

They could ask customers for their opinion of the decision made to see if they were happy about it and have not responded negatively towards it. (1 mark)

They could look at employees attendance records – if attendance at work had improved this would indicate that a decision was successful. (1 mark)

They could check if the objectives had been achieved; if the objective of what they intended to achieve was met this would mean the decision had been successful. (1 mark)

4. A company can set up a basic website without having to invest huge sums of money to do so. (1 mark) Companies can market their products towards customers all over the world (1 mark) who in turn can make a purchase 24/7. A company benefits from this because without a website, they would either need to employ staff to take orders or bookings over the telephone or face-to-face. (1 mark) However, a company losses out on being able to have personal contact with customers (1 mark) and is unable to respond to any queries immediately – this could lose customers. (1 mark) A company can communicate changes to products or advertise new products quickly which can be easily accessed by customers (1 mark), but this relies on the technology working effectively – computer or internet problems can occur. (1 mark)

Only a maximum of 4 marks out of 6 can be awarded for positive points.

Only a maximum of 4 marks out of 6 can be awarded for negative.

> **TOP EXAM TIP**
>
> You don't need an equal number of positive and benefit points in a discuss question to pick up the available marks for it.

5. Satisfying the needs of specific consumers (eg business) from a gap identified in the market. (1 mark) It involves providing a specialised product that has limited demand and little competition. (1 mark)

6. (a) Skimming requires a high price to be charged for a new product that is often unique. (1 mark) The high price can be charged because little competition exists due to the unique and exclusiveness of the product (1 mark) and this can result in high profits. (1 mark) If necessary, the organisation has the flexibility to be able to reduce the price of the product if competition enters the market at a later time. (1 mark)

> **TOP EXAM TIP**
>
> Questions can contain more than one command word eg "describe" and 'justify'. It is necessary to address both command words to gain full marks for the question.

> **HINT** Because the question has specifically asked for you to describe and justify the pricing strategy skimming, you must do this. You can't describe and justify a different pricing strategy.

> **HINT** A description of skimming and 3 justifications are required to achieve the marks for this question.

(b) **Any 6 from:**

Competitive pricing – the price of the product is similar to that of competitors. (1 mark)

Penetration pricing – the price of the product is set intentionally low at its launch in order to gain a large market share. (1 mark)

Premium pricing – high prices are charged for a product. (1 mark)

Destroyer pricing – the price of the product is intentionally low in order to force competition out of the market. (1 mark)

Promotional pricing – price of the product is low in the short-term by giving eg a discount for a short period of time. (1 mark)

Loss leader – the price charged for the product is lower than what it costs to manufacture or provide it. (1 mark)

> **TOP EXAM TIP**
>
> You must try to provide as much detail as you can in a description question. Adding examples where you can is a great idea.

Psychological pricing – his involves setting a price that makes customers think it is cheaper that what it actually is eg 99p rather than £1 or £1.99 rather than £2. (1 mark)

7. (a) Assessment centres allow an organisation to see applicants undertaking a variety of tasks in different situations. (1 mark)

Many large organisations have assessment centres where they get applicants to take part in role play exercises, team building activities, testing and making presentations. (1 mark)

At all points during the assessment centre, the organisation will be watching each applicant carefully and making a note of their communication, team work and problem solving skills. (1 mark)

By giving candidates the opportunity to demonstrate their skills in a variety of situations, the organisation can be more assured that they have chosen the best person for the job, compared to only using one method of selection. (1 mark)

> **HINT** As part of an assessment centre, candidates may have to undertake other methods of selection eg tests and interviews.

(b) Recruitment is about encouraging people to apply for a job vacancy whereas selection is concerned with choosing the best person for the job. (1 mark)

A job description contains information about the job (eg duties, responsibilities) whereas the person specification contains information about the type of person required to do the job. (1 mark)

A psychometric test assesses a job applicant's personality whereas an aptitude test assesses the natural ability of an applicant in eg literacy or numeracy. (1 mark)

> **TOP EXAM TIP**
>
> To be able to pick up one mark in a distinguish question, you need to make 2 points.

> **HINT** Recruitment and selection are different!

SECTION 2

1. (a) (i) **Any 2 from for 1 mark each:**

   To provide an efficient service to the local community
   To satisfy the needs of the local community
   To use money received from taxes in the best possible way

> **HINT** Local government is different from central government.

   (ii) **Any 2 from for 1 mark each:**

   Council taxes – money received by the local government for providing services to the public.

   Funding from central government – money received from the central government.

   Income generated from charging for services (eg leisure facilities) by the local government to members of the public.

> **HINT** The sources of finance for a public sector organisation will include different sources of finance (eg taxes) compared to a private sector organisation.

(b) (i) The product life cycle consists of 5 stages: development, introduction, growth, maturity/saturation and decline as shown in the following diagram

Figure 1 – *Product life cycle diagram*

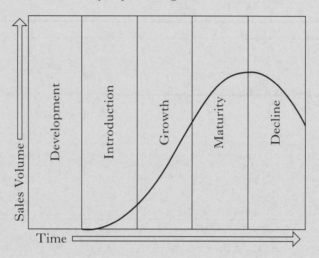

Marks are awarded for the diagram as follows:

- Correctly drawn and labelled axis – 1 mark
- 5 stages correctly identified on the diagram – 1 mark
- Correct product life cycle shape – 1 mark

During the development stage, organisations will carry out market research to identify the demand for a product, they may make a prototype of a product and may test the market's reaction to it. (1 mark) The product is then introduced to the market during which time the product is heavily advertised and sales will begin to grow. (1 mark) During the growth stage, because customers have a greater awareness of the product, sales are growing rapidly and a profit is beginning to be made. (1 mark) Once the product reaches the maturity stage, sales have peaked and the product is at its most profitable (1 mark). Once the product has saturated the market, sales will begin to decrease and eventually the product will become obsolete. (1 mark)

TOP EXAM TIP

Include diagrams in questions where you can (eg product life cycle, Boston box or stock management systems). This shows the Examiner that you do know each stage and may help you to remember what happens at each stage.

HINT It makes sense to describe each stage in the order that they occur.

(ii) The use of the product could be adapted eg new features added or a new flavour introduced. This would make the product more appealing to a wider range of customers as well as offering another reason for it to be purchased. (1 mark)

The packaging of the product could be improved, eg a new design or using more environmentally friendly materials. This would make the product stand out and people would take notice of it. (1 mark)

The name of the product could be changed to give it a new and improved image therefore encouraging people to buy it. (1 mark)

The way the product is promoted could be changed, eg increased advertising or celebrity endorsement. This will raise awareness of the product's existence and using new promotion methods may attract new customers who had not noticed it before. (1 mark)

Reducing the price of the product will enable more customers to buy it. The cheaper the product, the more affordable it is to a range of people. (1 mark)

> **HINT** As this is an explain question, development is required. It would not be enough to say 'The product could be adapted eg add new features' to gain marks.

(c) Organisations may prefer to recruit internally for a number of reasons. For example, existing employees are known by the organisation and will have shown whether they have the ability to do the job (1 mark) therefore reducing the chance of selecting the wrong person for the post. (1 mark) Employees recruited internally feel more valued and can become more motivated and productive to the organisation if they have been given the chance of promotion. (1 mark)

The organisation can save money on advertising the job, recruiting, selecting and training the new employee. (1 mark) As the existing employee is already familiar with the organisation's policies and procedures, there is no requirement to provide training on this. (1 mark)

(d) Having a quality recruitment and selection policy can help ensure that people with the skills and experience necessary to provide a high quality product/ service are selected and not those without. (1 mark)

Providing quality training programmes to all staff (eg training in using new machinery) will ensure they are capable of doing their jobs to the best of their ability. (1 mark)

Providing on-going support to staff (eg by having an appraisal system in place) will ensure development needs of staff are identified, which will mean they can do their job better. (1 mark)

> **HINT** This type of question is demanding. It requires you to think about 2 different topics and how they relate to each other.

2. (a) (i) Primary information is new information that has been gathered for a specific purpose by the organisation through conducting eg surveys or questionnaires. (1 mark)

Secondary information is second hand information from eg the internet or a newspaper that has been gathered for a different purpose. (1 mark)

(ii) Secondary information in cheaper to obtain than primary information because you do not need to eg train interviewers in conducting surveys or pay people to conduct surveys or interviews. (1 mark)

As it has already been gathered, the information already exists and is usually readily available on eg the internet. (1 mark)

As the information is readily available, it is less time consuming to collect compared to primary information. (1 mark)

(b) (i) Job production whereby a one off, unique product is made to the requirements and specification given by the customer. (1 mark)

Batch production involves a number of identical products being made at any one time and then the equipment could be changed or cleaned to produce an entirely different batch of products. (1 mark)

Flow production involves a product being built as it moves along an assembly line. As the product moves along the assembly line, parts are added until it is completed. (1 mark)

(ii) **Any 2 for one mark each:**

Type and nature of the product being made.
Amount of the product to be manufactured.
Methods of monitoring and ensuring quality.
Method of distribution.
Stock control management system.
Resources and technology available.

> **TOP EXAM TIP**
>
> Suggest questions do not require you to go into great depth in your answer.

(c) Quality management involves every person being committed to quality because the aim is to produce the perfect product. (1 mark) Team work and commitment is required at all levels of the organisation (1 mark) as is continual staff training and development. (1 mark) The organisation will be required to have policies that clearly define what quality is based on the important view of the customer. (1 mark) Quality management should result in the highest quality product that satisfies the customer. (1 mark)

> **HINT** Quality management was previously referred to as Total Quality Management (TQM).

(d) Poor industrial relations can result in employees striking meaning no work will be carried out and production will therefore stop. (1 mark) This could result in orders and deadlines being missed and therefore customers and repeat business being lost. (1 mark) The image and reputation of the organisation could become damaged which may put customers off purchasing from the organisation. (1 mark) Organisations who are known for poor industrial relations may find it difficult to recruit high quality employees because these people may be put off from applying for a vacancy. (1 mark)

> **HINT** The question has asked for the impact upon the organisation. Any reference to the impact upon employees would not receive any marks.

(e) A Trading, Profit and Loss Account shows a summary of the money that has came in and gone out of the organisation over a particular period of time. (1 mark)

The Trading Account shows the gross profit which is calculated by subtracting sales from cost of sales. (1 mark)

Cost of sales is the amount of money the organisation has spent before adding a profit margin to the goods being sold. (1 mark)

The Profit and Loss Account shows the net profit which is calculated by adding revenue received to the gross profit and then subtracting expenses. (1 mark)

The revenue received section includes all money received by the organisation eg rent received or discount received (1 mark) and the expenses section includes all money that has gone out of the organisation including wages, advertising and depreciation. (1 mark)

> **HINT** You will not be asked to prepare a Trading, Profit and Loss Account in this course, but you are required to have an understanding of the information they contain.

3 (*a*) One mark for each method given below:

Gender – products are targeted towards males or females.
Age – products are targeted towards people of a particular age eg clothing for children.
Income – people with higher incomes and social class are targeted with more sophisticated and/or luxurious products.
Religion – products are marketed towards people who have specific religious or cultural beliefs eg shops who specialise in selling foreign foods.
Geographical – products are marketed towards people who live in particular locations.

> **HINT** If you can think of examples of market segmentation this helps to strengthen your answer.

(*b*) (i) Decision making occurs at 3 levels: strategic, tactical and operational.

Strategic decisions are concerned with the long-term focus and direction of the organisation eg whether or not to expand into an overseas market. (1 mark)

Tactical decisions are medium-term decisions concerned with actions to achieve strategic decisions eg which premises to choose in a particular location when expanding abroad. (1 mark)

Operational decisions are ones that impact upon the day-to-day running of the organisation and only last for a short period of time. An example could be how many hours an employee will work next week. (1 mark)

> **TOP EXAM TIP**
> Examples strengthen your answers.

(ii) Employees who are allowed to participate in decision-making feel that their opinions and ideas matter and this can be motivating. (1 mark)

Change can be more easily introduced into an organisation if employees feel they have participated in the decision-making process. (1 mark)

Relationships between employer and employee will be improved if employees have participated in decision making and this could reduce the risk of poor employee relations and future industrial action. (1 mark)

(c) People will come together from various departments within the organisation to form the matrix structure and will each bring different skills and experiences to the benefit of the project. (1 mark) The skills of each member of the structure can be utilised effectively and they will each have the opportunity to work with other people who they can learn from and develop their own skills further. (1 mark) However, as every member of the structure has equal authority and responsibility, it can be difficult to coordinate activities being carried out. (1 mark) It can also prove expensive because often matrix structures require a separate team of administrative and support staff. (1 mark)

(d) The benefits of a strong corporate culture are that employees feel they belong and are part of the organisation which in turn can motivate staff which can improve efficiency and productivity in the organisation. (1 mark) Positive relationships can be created and maintained which helps improve employee relations. (1 mark) Employee loyalty can be increased which will help save on future recruitment costs (1 mark) and the image and identity of the organisation can be improved. (1 mark)

> **HINT** Corporate culture is sometimes referred to as organisation culture.

(e) **Any 3 from:**

A mortgage is a loan of money used to buy property that is secured against the property being purchased. (1 mark) Mortgages do not require to be paid back quickly and can be taken over a long period of time. (1 mark)

If the organisation is a limited company, it could issue extra shares to raise the necessary finance, provided it has not reached its authorised limit. (1 mark) Large amounts of finance can be raised this way as shareholders benefit from limited liability. (1 mark)

Venture Capitalists (or Business Angels) provide loans of money that are required to be paid back to organisations that are considered to be risky. (1 mark) Large loans can be obtained this way despite the fact that the organisation may have a poor credit history. (1 mark)

Sale and leaseback – organisations could sell their assets (eg equipment and machinery) to other companies and then lease (rent) these back. (1 mark) This allows them to obtain extra capital from the sale of the assets which in turn can be used to finance other investments. (1 mark)

> **TOP EXAM TIP**
>
> When a question has 2 command words eg Describe and Justify, you must address both in your answer to be able to gain full marks for that question.

> **HINT** This question requires you to think about sources of finance that will finance a long-term strategic decision. You must ensure the sources of finance you list are appropriate for the long term.

> **HINT** Questions may ask you for sources of finance appropriate to particular types of organisations. You need to be careful that you only write down sources appropriate to the type. For example, you could not say 'Issue debentures' as a source of finance for a sole trader or partnership.

4 (*a*) **Any 3 from:**

Cash budgets allows an organisation to identify when a deficit balance may occur which can give them the opportunity to take action to improve it. (1 mark)

Cash budgets allows an organisation to identify when a surplus balance may occur which can then allow them to invest this surplus into funding other activities. (1 mark)

Cash budgets from previous financial periods can be used to identify any trends (eg times when demand peaks or is particularly low) which can assist in production planning and decision making. (1 mark)

Because cash budgets are prepared in advance, it provides a target for an organisation or an individual department to work towards and therefore it encourages efficiency and methods of cutting costs to be considered and implemented. (1 mark)

> *HINT* Notice that each answer gives more of an explanation than simply an advantage of preparing a cash budget.

(*b*) (i) As stock only arrives when it is needed for production, money does not need to be paid out for it until it is required; this avoids money being tied up in stock. (1 mark)

As stock is received a short time before it is required, this saves on storage and security costs. (1 mark)

(ii) Discounts could be offered to customers who pay their bill within a short period of time. (1 mark) This will encourage customers to pay quickly and the money received can then be used to fund other activities. (1 mark)

By increasing advertising and promotion, more customers can be attracted and encouraged to make a purchase. (1 mark) More products being purchased increases sales and cash flow. (1 mark)

Assets that are no longer required could be sold to raise cash. (1 mark) Selling them will raise cash and because they are not required by the organisation it will not cause any disruption to the organisation's operations. (1 mark)

> **TOP EXAM TIP**
>
> Justify questions require you to give a reason to support your answer ie a reason why something should be chosen.

> *HINT* Notice that each description is given and then the justification follows on from it.

(*c*) There has been an increase in employment opportunities in the tertiary sector and a decrease in the primary/secondary sectors because of deindustrialisation. (1 mark)

More women are now in employment in both full-time and part-time jobs. (1 mark)

Developments in ICT have allowed more people to work out of the office either as homeworkers or teleworkers. (1 mark)

People have recognised the advantages of becoming self-employed and are opting to do this. (1 mark)

(d) Line relationships exist between a subordinate and their immediate line manager eg Marketing Assistant has a line relationship with the Marketing Manager. (1 mark)

Lateral relationships exist between people on the same level of the organisation structure eg Finance Manager and the Sales Manager. (1 mark)

Functional relationships exist when one department provides support or a service to another department. The Human Resources Department for example has a functional relationship with other departments when they provide support during the recruitment and selection process. (1 mark)

HINT Examples of different types of relationships are not essential to be awarded the mark, but do strengthen the answer.

(e) (i) Product endorsement is when organisations pay to have celebrities promote their product or service. (1 mark) An example would be David Beckham who has been associated with Pepsi and more recent Sharpies pens.

HINT An example would add value to your answer as shown above.

(ii) Product endorsement helps to promote a good image for the organisation (1 mark) as people often associate the celebrity with the product and therefore want to buy it. (1 mark) If the celebrity is very well known and successful it can therefore help the organisation increase its sales. (1 mark) However, it is an expensive method of promotion as celebrities do charge large sums of money for the work. (1 mark) The organisation must carefully ensure that it chooses the correct celebrity to promote the image of the product it wants to have otherwise it will not be as successful (1 mark) Finally, any negative publicity the celebrity has had or could have in the future can have a negative impact upon the sales of the product. (1 mark)

TOP EXAM TIP

You do not have to give equal numbers of costs and benefits to be able to pick up full marks for a question.

5. (a) (i) It can assist in decisions making because a large amount of information can be gathered. (1 mark)
Information can be collected easily and distributed to a large number of people. (1 mark)
Records can be maintained, edited and searched easily when required for decision making. (1 mark)
Communication with people over the world can be carried out eg through using videoconferencing without the need to travel. (1 mark)
It can assist in product design and manufacturing. (1 mark)

HINT The phrase 'invests heavily' basically means that an organisation spends lots of money on something.

> *HINT* — ICT is more than just using a computer. It includes using technology in manufacturing, communication and processing information.

(ii) **Any 4 from:**

Word processing software allows text to be entered, edited and presented in a suitable format eg to create a letter. (1 mark)

Database software allows a collection of related information to be stored, retrieved and edited quickly eg to keep records on customers. (1 mark)

Spreadsheet software allows numerical information to be stored, retrieved and edited quickly. It can be used to store financial information (eg sales figures) or stock levels. (1 mark)

Presentation software allows presentations to be created and shown electronically, usually through a projector onto a screen. (1 mark)

> **TOP EXAM TIP**
> Even if examples are not asked for, it strengthens your answer if you are able to provide them.

Computer Aided Design software allows products to be designed in 3D on a computer. (1 mark)

> *HINT* — Think about the packages you use during your studies and what you use them for. Sometimes you are only having to write down the obvious!

(b) The Computer Misuse Act 1990 exists to deter people from gaining unauthorised access to computer systems to commit crime. (1 mark)

The National Minimum Wage Regulations 1999 exist to ensure that employees are paid at least a certain amount of money per hour for their work so that organisations can not pay people too low an amount. (1 mark)

> **TOP EXAM TIP**
> Some questions require you to provide knowledge gained from different parts of the course.

The Race Relations Act 1976 aims to prevent the discrimination of people based on their colour, race, ethnic origin or religion. (1 mark)

(c) Training allows an employee to become more highly skilled in their work (1 mark), which can result in them being more highly motivated and productive. (1 mark) As a result, the quantity of products being wasted or scrapped is reduced and the cost associated with wastage reduced. (1 mark) An organisation who invests in staff training and development can contribute towards giving them a good name and reputation (1 mark) and the organisation can introduce change much more easily. (1 mark) However, training is expensive both financially (1 mark) and in the time lost when employees are being trained. (1 mark) Sometimes the organisation may also need to spend time persuading people to be trained if they are reluctant to undertake it because of the fear it will change their current ways of working. (1 mark) Finally, organisations need to be aware of the fact that those employees who have been highly trained may find a more highly paid job with another organisation. (1 mark) (*d*) **Any 4 from:**

A structured decision making model provides a systematic and structured approach to carrying out decision making. (1 mark)

No quick decisions are made because time is given to gather information. (1 mark)

Time is given to think about and consider the range of options (alternatives) available to the organisation. (1 mark)

The internal and external factors that may impact upon the decision can be considered provided time permits. (1 mark)

The effectiveness and impact of each decision on organisation is considered during the evaluation stage and strategies for improvement considered. (1 mark)

> **TOP EXAM TIP**
>
> Reading each question carefully is crucial in being able to answer it. So many marks can be lost by people not reading the question!

> **TOP EXAM TIP**
>
> Your Higher Business Management exam paper will always include questions from every topic in the course.

> HINT
>
> The structured decision making model contains different stages. However, this question has not asked you to describe each stage so it is unnecessary to do so.

SECTION 1

1. **Finance**
    * Weakened world markets.
    * 7% decrease in sales.
    * Turbulent economic conditions.
    * Rising costs.
    * Tax increases.
    * Future investors put off.

> **TOP EXAM TIP**
>
> Managing your time in exams is crucial. Read the instructions on your exam paper carefully and take note of the time you should spend on each section.

Human Resources
* Protests means negative consequences for Jonnie Walker brand.
* 900 job cuts.
* Employees disgruntled – impact on morale.

External
* Infrastructure limitations at Kilmarnock.
* United States stock reductions.
* Weakened world markets.
* Turbulent economic conditions.
* Tax increases.

1 mark per correctly identified problem
Maximum of 4 marks per heading
(10 marks maximum for question).

> **HINT**   Don't write down the problems you identify under any heading, or worse, all the headings. Think about what type of problem it is.

2. Political influences, such as new UK or international laws, can prevent or restrict an organisation from doing what they would like because the law has to be compiled with. (1 mark)

    Economic influences, such as an increased exchange rate, could prevent an organisation from trading with another country because of the cost of doing this is too high. (1 mark)

    Social influences such as changing cultures, trends and fashions make it difficult for organisations to predict what customers want and makes it difficult for them to satisfy the customer. (1 mark)

    Technological influences for example new technology make it difficult and expensive for organisations to keep up-to-date with technological advancements. (1 mark)

Environmental influences – unpredictable weather can impact upon the activities that organisations carry out and can mean plans have to change without notice. (1 mark)

Competition – an increase in competition from home and overseas can impact upon the decisions an organisation makes, as well as its customer base, meaning organisations have to find ways to stay ahead of competition. (1 mark)

HINT   A good way of remembering what the external influences on a business are is to remember the PESTEC acronym: Political, Economic, Social, Technological, Environmental and Competition.

3.   (a)   **Any 4 from:**

Merging with another business can eliminate competition from the market because 2 businesses have became one. (1 mark)

The business has gained the assets and resources (eg skills and knowledge) from the business they have merged with. (1 mark)

The share of the market that the business has is larger than what each company had individually. (1 mark)

The business can take advantage of economies of scale and obtain discounts for buying in larger quantities. (1 mark)

The business is now larger and is in a better position to be able to stand up to possible takeover bids by other organisations. (1 mark)

HINT   No marks are available for simply describing what a merger is.

(b)   Organisations can use integration to grow their business in a number of ways. Vertical integration occurs when a business joins with another business in the same industry but who are at a different stage in the production process. (1 mark) Backward vertical integration would occur if the business joined with a supplier (1 mark) and forward vertical integration would occur if the business joined with a customer. (1 mark) Horizontal integration would occur if the business joined with another business at the same stage of the production process as them. (1 mark)

HINT   Examples of integration could have been given to support the answer.

4.   Research the buyers market (eg by carrying out questionnaires) to find out what the customer wants. This is important in ensuring that the organisation provides the customer with what they want. (1 mark)

Research what similar products (if any) a competitor may have. Organisations want to ensure they have the competitive edge and by researching this they can ensure they develop a product that is better than an existing one. (1 mark)

List the resources that will be required to create and launch a new product and whether or not it has the resources necessary. If the organisation does not have the necessary resources (eg finance) then the product will not be successful. (1 mark)

Test the market's reaction to the new product so that any changes required can be identified and then made so that the product fully meets the customers' requirements and sales revenue can be made from it. (1 mark)

Promote and advertise the new product so that the customer is aware that it exists and can then buy it when it becomes available. (1 mark)

> **HINT** These activities take place before the product is launched onto the market. Once it is launched, the product life cycle begins.

5. Machinery can work for 24 hours a day, 7 days a week without a break whereas people can't. (1 mark)

Employing people can be cheaper than having to purchase expensive equipment. (1 mark)

People can use their initiative to solve problems whereas machinery can't. (1 mark)

The quality of work can vary when using people in the production process but machinery will produce a standardised and accurate product. (1 mark)

> **HINT** Capital production involves using machinery whereas labour intensive involves using humans in the production process. It is necessary to know this before you can correctly answer the question.

> **TOP EXAM TIP**
>
> When answering compare questions, you need to provide a direct comparison between the 2 variables to gain one mark.

6. **Any 6 from:**

Financial incentives (eg bonuses for meeting sales targets) could be provided as a way of encouraging workers to work harder and producing a better quality of work. (1 mark)

Social activities that involve members of the organisation coming together could be arranged as this makes them feel valued and they may enjoy socialising with their work colleagues outwith the working environment. (1 mark)

Allowing employees to take advantage of flexible working practices can motivate employees as it allows them to manage their work/life balance and juggle their work and personal commitments to suit their needs. (1 mark)

Providing training to employees so that they can improve their skills and performance in the work place make them feel valued and they may be motivated by this. (1 mark)

Consultation and communication with the workforce is crucial in maintaining good employee relations and they should be should be encouraged to express their views and opinions on matters and decisions that impact upon them. (1 mark)

Employees should be given regular positive feedback on their performance because praise is motivating. (1 mark)

> *HINT* Motivation is about how eager employees are to work hard and how much energy they have.

7. (a) Good public relations (PR) between a business and the public is essential because it is the key to good communication between them. (1 mark) Good PR will ensure that the business' name and image is maintained during any bad publicity or media reports and therefore help to maintain sales. (1 mark)

   (b) A press release could be issued – this is a written statement from an organisation to the press/media that tells people what the organisation is doing and the activities it is carrying out. (1 mark)

   The organisation could make a donation (a sum of money) to a charity and publicise the fact that it is doing this. (1 mark)

   The organisation could improve its image by becoming 'green' and being active in reducing carbon emissions and having a commitment towards recycling. (1 mark)

8. (a) Maximum stock level – the maximum amount of stock at any one time. This cannot be too high because the organisation would not have the facilities to store stock above this level. (1 mark)

   Minimum stock level – the minimum quantity of stock at any one time. This cannot be too low or the organisation may not be able to continue manufacturing its product. (1 mark)

   Re-order level – the quantity of stock at which more stock is ordered. This is important because too low a level will mean that the organisation may not have enough raw materials if there was a delay in the raw materials being delivered. (1 mark)

   Re-order quantity – the quantity of stock to be ordered to bring levels back to the maximum stock level. This should take into account maximum stock level so that the total stock does not go above this. (1 mark)

> *HINT* You could draw a stock control management diagram to help support your answer.

   (b) Stock can automatically be reordered when the reorder quantity is reached. (1 mark)

A computerised system can quickly provide information to managers on the quantity of stock available for each product. (1 mark)

SECTION 2

1. (a) Skills, ability and experience of staff – they need to have sufficient knowledge and experience of what they are making to produce a quality product. (1 mark)

   The standard of equipment or machinery being used – if these are of poor quality or in need of upgrading, this will result in a poorer product being produced. (1 mark)

   The quality of raw materials – poor quality raw materials will result in a poor quality product being produced. (1 mark)

   The financial cost of providing a quality product or service – the more expensive it is for an organisation to provide the resources to make a quality product may result in cheaper or fewer methods of quality being used. (1 mark)

   (b) The purpose of a mission statement is to communicate to staff and employees (1 mark) a summary of the aims/objectives/focus of the organisation. (1 mark)

HINT ▷ Two points need to be given to obtain the 2 marks for the question.

   (c) (i) Written information – this is information presented in the form of text, eg a letter or memo (1 mark)

       Verbal information – this is information presented orally through eg a conversation or presentation (1 mark)

       Numerical information – this is information in number form eg in a spreadsheet. (1 mark)

       Pictorial information – this is information presented through a photograph or picture. (1 mark)

       Graphical information – this is information presented through a chart or graph. (1 mark)

       The 5 types of information above are the main types, but also acceptable would be:

       Quantitative information – this is information that can be measured or counted. It would presented in numerical form. (1 mark)

Qualitative information – this is information in the form of words that is descriptive and/or contains the opinions of other people. (1 mark)

TOP EXAM TIP

No marks are awarded for simply identifying.

HINT   This is an ideal question to use examples to support your answer.

(ii) Primary information is first hand information collected for a specific purpose. (1 mark) Because it is collected for a specific purpose it is relevant (1 mark) and is more up-to-date than existing secondary information. (1 mark) The organisation who has collected it will know where the information has came from (1 mark) but they do not know if it will contain bias or if the responses by individuals who provided it are truthful. (1 mark) It will also have been time consuming (1 mark) and expensive to obtain if interviews or surveys had been conducted. (1 mark) The reliability of the research will also be doubtful if too small a sample was used when the information was been gathered. (1 mark)

TOP EXAM TIP

Costs are disadvantages and benefits are advantages.

HINT   Costs and benefits need to be considered in this question.

(d) The aim or purpose of promotion activities is to raise awareness to the customer that a product or organisation actually exists – it tells them that it is available through eg advertising. (1 mark) Promotion activities may encourage people to buy a product by offering a discount or special offer (1 mark). Finally, it encourages loyalty and repeat purchases by customers. (1 mark)

(e) Centralised decisions are made by Senior Management of a company with little involvement from lower level managers whereas decentralised decision making occurs further down the hierarchy by managers who have had this power delegated to them. (1 mark)

Centralised decision making is associated with tall hierarchical structures whereas decentralised decision making is associated with flatter structures. (1 mark)

TOP EXAM TIP

Use phrases such as 'whereas', 'on the other hand' and 'however' to make your comparison between 2 or more factors.

Centralised decision making involves Senior Management telling other people what to do and how to carry it out but on the other hand, decentralised decision making allows for the ideas and skills of other people to be used which in turn can motivate them. (1 mark)

2. (a) **Any 5 from (1 mark each):**

Too much money is being tied up in stock.

Too much time is being given to customers to pay their debt (a long credit period).
Not enough money is being made from sales.
Too short a credit period is being offered by creditors or suppliers.
The value of drawings taken out by the owners has been high.
Money is being spent on large capital items.

(b) (i) Functional grouping – grouping by department, eg Marketing, Human Resources, Operations, Finance, Research & Development. (1 mark)

Grouping by product or service. This is when activities are grouped based upon the products that the organisation sells. (1 mark)

Geographical grouping (also known as territory grouping). This involves grouping activities based on particular geographical locations. (1 mark)

Customer grouping – grouping by type of customer. (1 mark)

Technology grouping – used by manufacturing companies to group activities according to the production process used. (1 mark)

HINT ▷ If time permitted, you could draw small diagrams to illustrate what each grouping would look like.

(ii) The size of the organisation; smaller organisations would for example be unlikely to have a territory grouping because it will mainly focus on selling its product in a small geographical location. (1 mark)

The product or service being sold may be more suited to one particular activity grouping or another. Organisations who offer a variety of products will be more suited to having a product or service grouping than an organisation who only sells one type of product. (1 mark)

The market in which the organisation operates; organisations who cater for a variety of market segments would be more suitable for grouping by customer than those who cater for one type of customer. (1 mark)

The amount of technology used in the organisation's activities may make it more or less suitable for grouping by technology. Large manufacturing organisations tend to find this grouping more suitable because they group their activities according to the technology being used. (1 mark)

(c) Public corporations are owned by the government (1 mark) and are controlled by a Chairperson and Board of Directors. (1 mark)

> **HINT**   A public corporation is part of the public sector – it does not have profit making as its main motive. Do not confuse it with a Public Limited Company which belongs to the private sector.

(d) (i) Information from desk research is inexpensive to obtain because a lot of it is available freely from internet websites. (1 mark)

Because desk research already exists, it is easier to obtain than carry out field research. (1 mark)

The organisation does not need to train staff to design and carry out surveys or interviews. (1 mark)

(ii) An observation involves watching something and recording what happens. (1 mark) It could involve the observer counting how many times something happens, someone does something or what someone's reaction is to a particular situation. (1 mark) As those being observed may be unaware they will react to a situation or scenario in a more natural and spontaneous way. (1 mark) The information that is obtained through observation – quantitative information – can be analysed more easily compared to qualitative (1 mark) because no feelings or judgement are obtained from the person being observed. (1 mark) However, the drawback to this is that those being observed cannot be asked to comment or give an opinion on why they did or did not do something and this may be a useful piece of information that the company would benefit from. (1 mark)

3. (a) Information and promotional material on the product may be provided by the wholesaler, therefore saving the retailer resources of having to provide or create this. (1 mark)

Smaller retailers might be able to take advantage of credit facilities and delivery terms, which enables them to more effectively manage their cash flow position. (1 mark)

Retailers do not have to pay for expensive storage facilities because the wholesaler will sell smaller quantities to the retailer compared to obtaining the product directly from the manufacturer. (1 mark)

(b) Random sampling – randomly selecting people from a list, eg telephone book or electoral roll, and then telephoning these people. People who are chosen from the list to take part in the survey must be contacted. (1 mark)

Stratified random sampling – the sample is based on segments of how the population as a whole is divided. (1 mark)

Quota sampling – selecting a number of people to question based on certain characteristics (eg age, occupation, gender). (1 mark) (*c*) The purpose of the Data Protection Act is to govern the way organisations collect, store, process and distribute information. (1 mark) Its principles are below. (1 mark each)

- Data should be obtained and processed fairly.
- Data can only be held for specific and lawful purposes.
- Data held should be adequate, relevant and not excessive for the purpose.
- Data should be accurate and up to date.
- Data should not be held longer than is necessary.
- Individuals are entitled access to the data held about them.
- If appropriate the data should be altered to ensure it is accurate or deleted if no longer necessary.
- Security of the data should be maintained to ensure no unlawful access to the data can take place.

(*d*) Interest:

Want jobs in the local area. (1 mark)
Want to ensure the organisation does not damage or pollute the environment. (1 mark)
Want to receive social benefits (eg better roads and housing). (1 mark)

Influence:
Can make complaints to the local council. (1 mark)
Can participate in protests. (1 mark)
Can provide positive or negative feedback about the organisation. (1 mark)

(*e*) (i) Preparing a cash budget allows an organisation to:

Identify when a negative cash balance (a deficit) may occur so that appropriate action can be taken. (1 mark)

Identify when a positive cash balance (a surplus) may occur as this could be used to finance other investments and make future decisions. (1 mark)

Have the time to arrange additional sources of finance if a cash flow problem may occur in the future. (1 mark)

Make decisions based on previous and forecasted ones because these could be used to identify trends eg seasonal fluctuations in demand. (1 mark)

> **HINT** Remember that a cash budget is a forecast into the organisation's future cash flow position.

> **TOP EXAM TIP**
>
> **Explain** questions require more development than a **describe** question.

(ii) Liquidity – how able an organisation is to pay its short-term debts. (1 mark)

Trade credit – this method of finance allows an organisation to purchase goods and pay for them later. (1 mark)

Fixed assets – these are items that the organisation owns that will last for longer than one year eg motor vehicles or premises. (1 mark)

> **TOP EXAM TIP**
>
> In this course you will not be asked to **prepare** a set of accounts or to **calculate** ratios.

4. (a) A strong brand allows the organisation and/or its products to be easily recognised (1 mark). Strong brand names are often associated with a good quality product (1 mark), which in turn can lead to an increased loyalty established between the organisation and its customers. (1 mark) The time that takes to establish this loyalty can be long however (1 mark) and also the cost of exposing customers to the brand through advertising and promotion can be high. (1 mark) Because a strong brand is often associated with high quality, the organisation can command a higher price for its product than without it (1 mark). However, because of the associated high quality, sometimes other companies will try to copy the brand and will produce fakes or products that look very similar. (1 mark) Finally, when the organisation is attempting to introduce new and similar products to the market a strong brand identity means that they can often do this much more successfully compared to an organisation without it (1 mark) but if the product was very different from what they are known for, it can be difficult to introduce new products to the market. (1 mark)

> **HINT** You will not pick up any marks for simply giving examples of brands.

> **TOP EXAM TIP**
>
> You need to discuss advantages <u>and</u> disadvantages to be able to pick up full marks in a discuss question.

(b) **Any 7 from:**

Information must be timely – this means that it is available when it is needed and is the most up-to-date information available. (1 mark)

It must be accurate, which means that it is error free. (1 mark)

It must be appropriate, which means suitable and relevant to the decision being made or task being carried out. (1 mark)

It must be objective, which means it is bias free. (1 mark)

It must concise – brief, straight to the point and free from 'waffle' (1 mark) but at the same time sufficient, meaning there is enough of it to make the decision. (1 mark)

It must be available – it should be obtained as easily as possible. (1 mark)

It must be cost effective – the cost of obtaining the information should be less than value that it will be provide. (1 mark)

(c) Entrepreneurs are willing to the take the risk of losing their own money in pursuit of developing a business idea. (1 mark)

They are known and associated with creativity, unusual ideas and being innovative. (1 mark)

They combine the factors of production (land, labour, capital and enterprise) to make a business idea successful. (1 mark)

They use their initiative (follow their instincts) in decision making and problem solving. (1 mark)

> **HINT** Do not get yourself confused with an entrepreneur and an entrepreneurial structure.

(d) (i) Homeworkers work from home whereas teleworkers workout with the office but not necessarily at home (eg travelling sales people on the move). (1 mark)

Temporary contracts do not have a specific end date when the employee will finish working whereas fixed-term contracts will have a specific end date. (1 mark)

> **HINT** Homeworkers and teleworkers are different.

(ii) **Any 3 from:**

Staff are generally more motivated and are therefore more productive. (1 mark)

There will be a reduced number of absences and incidents of late coming. (1 mark)

Space and money can be saved in the office if employees are working out of the office. (1 mark)

Potential employees may be attracted to an organisation who can offer flexible working practises, so an organisation can recruit higher quality staff more easily. (1 mark)

5. (a) (i) Decision making can become quicker because information can be processed much more quickly than manually using ICT. (1 mark)

The quantity of information that can be accessed through eg the internet is large and can improve decision making as more information is available in order to make an informed decision. (1 mark)

Decisions can be communicated more easily and quickly by eg the internet or e-mail to employees and customers than by letter or telephone. (1 mark)

"What if" scenarios can be modelled on spreadsheet software allowing the organisation to see what would happen if a particular decision was made. (1 mark)

Large quantities of data and information can be displayed in chart form allowing trends and patterns to be seen. (1 mark)

Packages eg spreadsheet and project management software, could be used to monitor the progress of decisions and tasks being undertaken ensuring that deadlines are met. (1 mark)

> HINT   Your answer must relate to why ICT would help decision making.

(ii) A decision would be effective if it had solved the problem it was designed to solve and in the process contributed towards achieving the organisation's objectives. (1 mark)

The level of profit (or loss) would be an indicator into a successful decision.

More profit being made (or lower the loss) would suggest that a decision has been successful. (1 mark)

A decrease in the number of employees not reporting to work would indicate that a decision was successful. (1 mark)

Employees could be asked through a questionnaire if they feel morale in the workforce had improved, and if it had this would suggest decision making was being successful. (1 mark)

(b) In order to produce a quality product or service, organisations needs to ensure that the inputs to the production process such as raw materials, employees and the equipment to be used are of a high quality. (1 mark) The use of highly skilled, qualified and trained staff who are appropriately supervised is also important. (1 mark)

Quality assurance requires products to be checked at various stages during production. (1 mark) Any product that does not meet the standard that is expected by the organisation will be disregarded. (1 mark)

Quality Management involves the whole organisation (including the workforce) where commitment to quality is second to nature. (1 mark) The organisation beliefs that no errors are acceptable and that a perfect product should be produced at all times. (1 mark)

Quality control involves checking products at the end of the manufacturing process. (1 mark)

Benchmarking involves comparing the organisation's product with the best they can find in the market in an attempt to match standards. (1 mark)

(c) A balance sheet shows the worth of an organisation. (1 mark)

It contains clear sections on:

The value of fixed assets – those items of value that will last the organisation for a long period of time eg premises. (1 mark)

The value of current assets – those items of value that will not last the organisation for a long period of time usually under one year eg stock. (1 mark)

The total value of current liabilities – the short term debts that the organisation has eg short term loans. (1 mark)

TOP EXAM TIP

Examples are not essential but always help to strengthen an answer.

How the organisation has been financed. (1 mark)

(d) The organisation can ask the applicant very specific questions. (1 mark)

Because every applicant for the same job will have completed the same application form, it is easier to make comparisons between applicants. (1 mark)

Application forms can be completed (and sometimes submitted) electronically. (1 mark)

HINT   An application form is different from a Curriculum Vitae.

SECTION 1

1. **Finance**
    - Economic downturn.
    - Increasing operating (eg fuel) costs.
    - Falling share prices.
    - Lost revenue on refunding cancelled trips to Mexico.

    Marketing
    - Consumers watching their money.
    - Demand is down/passenger numbers fall.
    - Competition from local/cheaper holidays.

    External
    - Rising consumer unemployment.
    - Economic downturn.
    - High fuel costs/duty.
    - Tough winter conditions.
    - Concerns over merger of British Airways and Spain's Iberia.
    - Outbreak of swine flu.

    1 mark per correctly identified problem.
    Maximum of 4 marks per heading.
    10 marks maximum for question.

> **TOP EXAM TIP**
>
> This section should take you no more than 1 hour 15 minutes to complete.

2. Having a large quantity of unused (or unsold) stock means that cash is being tied up unnecessarily that could be used for other purposes. (1 mark)
    Too much time is being given to customers to pay their debt (a long credit period) and therefore the business is not receiving money from them for a while. (1 mark)
    Not enough money is being made from the selling of stock and therefore there is little cash being raised this way. (1 mark)
    Too short a credit period being offered by creditors or suppliers and therefore cash is being given to them quickly. (1 mark)
    The value of drawings taken out by the owners of the company has been too high. (1 mark)
    Large amounts of money have been spent on purchasing fixed assets and large. (1 mark)

3. (a) A merger happens when two businesses of approximately the same size, agree to become one.

> *HINT* > A merger is not the same as a takeover or a demerger.

(b) A merger allows a company to wipe out a competitor and at the same time increasing their market share because 2 companies have became one. (1 mark)

Because the 2 companies are now one, they can share the assets that each other have. (1 mark)

Because the company is now much larger, they can order larger quantities of materials and other items and take advantage of economies of scale. (1 mark)

> **TOP EXAM TIP**
>
> Be careful to read questions carefully because sometimes they might ask for advantages or disadvantages only.

4. Political influences such as new UK or international laws can prevent or restrict an organisation from doing what they would like. (1 mark)

Economic influences, such as increased interest rates, means companies can no longer afford to trade and do business with other companies in different countries. (1 mark)

Social influences, such as changing cultures, trends and fashions, make it difficult for organisations to predict what customers what. (1 mark)

Technological influences for example new technology make it difficult for organisations to keep up-to-date with technological advancements. (1 mark)

Environmental influences – unpredictable weather can impact upon the activities that organisations carry out. (1 mark)

Competition – an increase in competition from home and overseas can impact upon the decisions an organisation makes as well as its customer base. (1 mark)

5. (a) Gender – specific holidays being targeted towards males or females. (1 mark)

Age – holidays are targeted towards people of a particular age eg Club 18-30 holidays for those in this age group. (1 mark)

Income – people with higher incomes and social class are targeted with more sophisticated and/or luxurious holiday packages. (1 mark)

Religion – products are marketed towards people who have specific religious or cultural beliefs eg holidays to countries with religious connections. (1 mark)

Geographical – holidays are marketed towards people who live in particular locations. (1 mark)

> **HINT** It is always a good idea to give examples where you can. In this question, you can give examples that are related to the question.

(b) Functional grouping – grouping by departments, eg human resources, marketing, finance and operations. (1 mark)

Grouping by product or service. This is when activities are grouped based upon the products that the organisation sells. (1 mark)

Geographical grouping (also known as territory grouping). This involves grouping activities based on particular geographical locations. (1 mark)

Technology grouping – used by manufacturing companies to group activities according to the production process used. (1 mark)

6. (a) Organisations make 3 types of decisions, known as strategic, tactical and operational. Strategic decisions are long-term decisions that set the vision for the organisation (1 mark) and because they impact upon the whole organisation, they are made by Senior Management. (1 mark) The next type of decision is tactical. These decisions are medium-term decisions that put into place actions to achieve strategic decision (1 mark). Because these decisions are not as long-term as strategic ones, they are made by middle management. (1 mark). Finally, operational decisions are day-to-day decisions that only impact upon the organisation in the short term. (1 mark) These decisions would be made by low level managers. (1 mark)

> **HINT** Remember – decision making takes place at 3 levels: strategic, tactical and operational.

(b) A structured decision making model provides a systematic and structured approach to carrying out decision making. (1 mark)

No quick decisions are made because time is given to gather information. (1 mark)

Time is given to think about and consider the range of options (alternatives) available to the organisation. (1 mark)

The internal and external factors that may impact upon the decision can be considered provided time permits. (1 mark)

The effectiveness and impact of each decision on organisation is considered during the evaluation stage and strategies for improvement considered. (1 mark)

> **HINT** Don't waste time writing down the stages of the decision-making model because the question does not ask for them.

7. Products can be transported across the world fairly quickly compared to other methods eg sea because air travel is quick. (1 mark)

Large amounts of small products can be transported by air because aircrafts are capable of holding large amounts rather than having several lorries transporting smaller amounts. (1 mark)

The cost of transporting products by air is expensive. (1 mark)

> **HINT** Channels of distribution are different from methods of distribution such as rail, road, sea and air.

Products still need to be transported to an airport, which could be expensive because another method of transport (eg road) would need to be used to get them to the airport. (1 mark)

Large products cannot be transported by air because aircrafts do not have the size capacity to hold large items. (1 mark)

SECTION 2

1. (a) (i) Manufacturer to Customer. (1 mark)

Manufacturer to Retailer to Customer. (1 mark)

Manufacturer to Wholesaler to Customer. (1 mark)

Manufacturer to Wholesaler to Retailer to Customer. (1 mark)

> **TOP EXAM TIP**
>
> Read over all the questions in section 2 quickly before deciding which 2 to answer. You don't have enough time to start a question and then decide you can't answer it.

(ii) Cost – the financial cost of actually distributing the product needs to be kept to the absolute minimum. (1 mark)

Demand location – where the customer actually is needs to be considered and the impact of seasonal demand. (1 mark)

Type of product – the actually product being sold needs to be transported in the best possible way eg fresh products need to be transported quickly so they do not go off. (1 mark)

The law – pieces of legislation can determine whether or not a product can be sold in a particular place. (1 mark)

(b) (i) Facilitator role – the provision and delivery of management training and guidance will be done by the HRM department. (1 mark)

Auditor role – HRM policies and procedures must be followed by all those in the organisation and the HRM department will monitor and report on this. (1 mark)

Consultancy role – specialist information and guidance will be given by the HRM department to managers on handling different matters and particular situations. (1 mark)

Executive role – the HRM department are experts on employment and HR matters. (1 mark)

Service role – the HRM department must ensure that all employees and management are kept up-to-date with changes in HR information, procedures and law. (1 mark)

HINT > You can remember the role of HR by trying to remember the acronym FACES.

(ii) A one-to-one interview is when one interviewer interviews a candidate whereas a panel interview is when more than one interviewer interviews a candidate. (1 mark)

A one-to-one interview would see the interviewer asking all of the questions whereas a panel interview would see each interviewer asking at least one question each. (1 mark)

A one-to-one interview has the disadvantage that the person interviewing could show favouritism or bias towards a particular candidate whereas in a panel interview because more than one interviewer is involved, this is less likely to happen. (1 mark)

> **TOP EXAM TIP**
>
> The word 'whereas' can be used to compare one point against another when answering a compare question.

(c) Financial incentives (eg bonuses for meeting sales targets) could be provided as a way of encouraging employees to work hard and meet targets. (1 mark)

Social activities that involve members of the organisation coming together could be arranged. (1 mark)

Allowing employees to take advantage of flexible working practices such as homeworking where employees can work from home. (1 mark)

Providing training to employees so that they can improve their skills and performance at work. (1 mark)

Encourage employee to participate in Quality Circles and/or Works Councils. (1 mark)

Employees should be given regular positive feedback on their performance and where necessary improvements that need to be made for example through an appraisal system. (1 mark)

(d) The Gross Profit % ratio shows us the % profit earned from selling products whereas the Net Profit % ratio shows the % profit earned from selling products when other expenses have been taken into account. (1 mark)

The Working Capital shows the ability of an organisation to pay its short-term debts whereas the Acid Test ratio shows the ability of the organisation in a crisis or unexpected situation to pay off its short-term debts. (1 mark)

> **TOP EXAM TIP**
>
> Distinguish questions require you to point out the differences between the topics you are discussing.

(e) E-mail can be used to send written messages (eg information to staff or to customers) from one person to another person or group of people quickly and instantly by simply typing in their e-mail address(s) into an e-mail sending program. (1 person)

Attachments (eg files and documents) can be sent to people quickly without the need to send these as hard copy documents through the post or by hand delivery. (1 mark)

2. (a) Time rate – employees are paid per hour worked and the more hours worked by the employee the more pay they will receive whereas flat rate – employees are paid a set amount per year which is divided into twelve equal monthly payments. (1 mark)

Piece rate – employees are paid per item produced normally in addition to a low flat rate whereas overtime – after working a set number of hours, overtime is paid for the extra hours worked. (1 mark)

Commission - Commission is usually a % of the sales value the employee has made and the amount of commission an employee receives depends on the value of sales they have made whereas a bonus is an additional payment an employee might get, eg for exceeding productivity targets. It will be paid in addition to their flat rate. (1 mark)

(b) The purpose of the Sex Discrimination Act is to ensure people regardless of their gender are treated the same and fairly. (1 mark)

The purpose of the Data Protection Act is to ensure organisations who store information about individuals do so in a lawful manner. It governs the way organisations collect, store, process and distribute information. (1 mark)

The purpose of the Health & Safety at Work Act is to protect the health and safety of people in the workplace by laying down responsibilities of the employee and employer. (1 mark)

The purpose of the Equal Pay Act is to ensure that men and women receive the same pay for doing work considered of the same (or equal) value.

HINT The question clearly asks you for the purpose of each piece of legislation and not its main principles or features.

(c) (i) A franchise exists when a business provides a product/service that has been supplied by another business. (1 mark) The 'new' business (the franchisee) will use the name and image of the original business (the franchisor). (1 mark)

HINT McDonalds, Burger King and Pizza Hut are examples of a franchise. You could include these as examples in your answer.

(ii) Advantages:

The franchisee provides a sum of money (which is usually a percentage of turnover) each year to the franchisor because the franchisee is operating under the franchisor's business name. (1 mark)

Risk is shared between the franchisee and franchisor and if the business was to get into problems, the risk is split between both. (1 mark)

The share of the market held by the franchisor can be increased without them having to invest additional capital into the business because this is provided by the franchisee. (1 mark)

Disadvantages:

If the franchisor had opened the business themselves, they may have received more revenue compared to that generated by the franchisee. (1 mark)

If a franchisee is operating poorly this could damage the name and image of the franchisor at no fault of their own. (1 mark)

> **HINT** The question specifically asks for the advantages and disadvantages for the franchisor and not the franchisee.

(d) The quality of the raw materials received from a supplier will determine the quality of the final product. (1 mark)

The reliability of the supplier is important in being able to meet deadlines and customer orders. (1 mark)

An organisation could lose money if production had to stop because raw materials were not delivered on time. (1 mark)

(e) **Product**

Selling the correct product is very important because people will not buy something they do not want. (1 mark) The organisation must carry out market research to identify what customers want because the more products an organisation sells, the better chance they have of maximising sales. (1 mark)

Price

The price of the product must reflect its quality and the demand for it but at the same time, allow the organisation to cover its costs and make a profit. (1 mark) It must not be too low or too high in comparison to the price of competitors because if it is too low an organisation would not be maximising sales revenue and if it is too high customers will go elsewhere. (1 mark)

Place

Customers need to be able to access the product so that they can buy it. (1 mark) How the product actually gets to the customer (the route it takes) is important because some products need to get to the customer quickly eg fresh produce so that it remains fresh. (1 mark)

Promotion

Promotion is about letting customers know that products exist so that they will purchase them. (1 mark) Organisations can also use other aspects of promotion (eg special offers) to entice customers to make a purchase that they might not have otherwise. (1 mark)

> **HINT** The question has not asked you to describe each element of the marketing mix so you do not need to do this. It would be wasting your time if you did this because the question does not ask for it!

3. (a) **Any 4 for one mark each:**

Written – is written down using text eg letters, memos, reports, newspaper articles.

Oral/Verbal – is spoken and then heard eg discussions, interviews, presentations.

Pictorial – this is information presented through pictures or photos.

Graphical – this is information presented through a chart or graph.

Numerical – information presented through numbers eg on a spreadsheet.

Quantitative – this information is factual and can be counted or measured.

Qualitative – this information includes opinions, views and judgements.

> *HINT* Sources and types of information are different. This question has asked you for types of information.

(b) The Computer Misuse Act is concerned with those people who intend to or have committed the offence of hacking into computer systems. (1 mark)

The Act makes it illegal for people to gain access to computer material without permission (1 mark), to gain unauthorised access with intent to commit or facilitate commission of further offences (1 mark) and it to modify computer material without permission. (1 mark)

(c) Employees feel they belong and are part of the organisation. (1 mark)
Efficiency and productivity for the organisation can increase. (1 mark)
Positive relationships can be created and maintained which helps improve employee relations. (1 mark)
Employee loyalty can be increased. (1 mark)
Image and identity of the organisation can be improved. (1 mark)

(d) Primary information is newly gathered information, whereas secondary information already exists. (1 mark)

Primary information is gathered for a specific purpose whereas secondary information has been gathered for a different purpose than what it will now be used for. (1 mark)

Primary information includes information gathered from field research eg questionnaires and observations, whereas secondary information includes information gathered from desk research eg from newspapers or website. (1 mark)

> **TOP EXAM TIP**
> Distinguish – look for the differences between 2 or more factors.

> *HINT* Sources of information are different from types of information.

(e) (i)   Taking industrial action such as a strike and therefore causing production and workflow to stop. (1 mark)

Not producing products or providing services to the standard expected thereby causing an increase in complaints by unhappy customers. (1 mark)

Leaving their job at the organisation to work for a competitor and causing a vacancy to be filled and shortage of staff until a replacement is found. (1 mark)

HINT > The question has asked for the influence of employees on an organisation and not their interest in the organisation.

(ii)   Customers are interested in an organisation because they want:
High quality products to be provided by the organisation. (1 mark)
The organisation to keep prices low on the products they are buying. (1 mark)
To receive a good standard of customer service and after sales service. (1 mark)

The Government is interested in an organisation because:
They want jobs to be provided for the people in the country. (1 mark)
They want money from the organisation through taxation. (1 mark)
They want communities to benefit from the social and economic benefits that business brings. (1 mark)

The local community is interested in an organisation because:
They want jobs to be provided by the organisation. (1 mark)
They want to ensure the organisation does not harm the environment surrounding it by its business activities. (1 mark)
They want to receive the social (eg improved roads) and economic benefits from the business. (1 mark)

Maximum of 2 marks per stakeholder.
Must be a different interest for each stakeholder.

HINT > This question asks specifically for external stakeholders.

4. (a)   Job production whereby a one off, unique product is made to the requirements and specification given by the customer. (1 mark)

Batch production involves a number of identical products being made at any one time and then the equipment could be changed or cleaned to produce an entirely different batch of products. (1 mark)

Flow production involves a product being built as it moves along an assembly line. As the product moves along the assembly line, parts are added until it is completed. (1 mark)

> **HINT** Examples of products manufactured using each type of production method would not be given a mark but would add value to your answer.

(b) Competition from overseas has increase where products can be produced at a cheaper cost than in the UK. (1 mark)

Customers have changed in terms of the products and services they demand and this has meant business has had to change if they want to satisfy the customers wants. (1 mark)

New government policies and laws have meant businesses have had to change in order to comply with this. (1 mark)

(c) Skimming – a high price to be charged for a new product that is often unique with little competition in the market whereas competitive pricing – the price of the product is similar to that of competitors. (1 mark)

Penetration pricing – the price of the product is set intentionally low at its launch in order to gain a large market share whereas premium pricing – high prices are charged for a product. (1 mark)

Destroyer pricing – the price of the product is intentionally low in order to force competition out of the market whereas promotional pricing - price of the product is low in the short-term by giving eg a discount for a short period of time. (1 mark)

Loss leader – the price charged for the product is lower than what it costs to manufacture or provide it whereas psychological pricing - his involves setting a price that makes customers think it is cheaper that what it actually is eg 99p rather than £1 or £1.99 rather than £2. (1 mark)

(d) (i) Decision making occurs at the centre of the organisation by the owner, with little input from employees. (1 mark)

> **HINT** Do not confuse entrepreneurial structures with the role of the entrepreneur.

(ii) Advantages (max 2 marks):
Quicker decision making. (1 mark)
A standardised approach to decision making with no conflict. (1 mark)

Disadvantages (max 2 marks):
Employees can become demotivated. (1 mark)
The best decision may be made because few people have had an input. (1 mark)

(*e*) (i) Public sector organisations are owned by the taxpayer (1 mark) but managed by the Government (1 mark) and consist of 3 types of organisations: Central Government, Local Government and Public Corporations. (1 mark)

Central Government is controlled by elected politicians and deal with issues affecting the whole country eg health service. (1 mark) Local Government for example, the local council, is controlled by elected politicians who have appointed managers to run the Local Government. They deal with issues such as schools and roads. (1 mark) Public corporations provide goods and services to the public and is managed by a Chairperson and Board of Directors. (1 mark)

> **HINT** Public sector organisations are different from Public Limited Companies who operate in the Private sector!

(ii) To provide an efficient service to the local community. (1 mark)
To satisfy the needs of the local community. (1 mark)
To use money received from taxes in the best possible way. (1 mark)
To stick within agreed and allocated budgets. (1 mark)

5. (*a*) (i) Benchmarking involves the organisation comparing their product with that of the market leader – this allows them to compare their product with the best in the industry to see if they can match this standard. (1 mark)

Quality assurance involves checking the product at various stages of the production process to attempt to reduce wastage by finding substandard products during production and not after. (1 mark)

Quality circles – where people in the organisation who are actually producing the products meet with management to find ways of solving problems so that their first hand experience can feed into this process. (1 mark)

> **TOP EXAM TIP**
> Remember – **explain** is more than a description!

(ii) Quality inputs are required to produce a quality output. (1 mark)
To achieve high sales revenue and make profit. (1 mark)
To ensure the organisation's reputation does not suffer. (1 mark)
To encourage customers to purchase their product. (1 mark)

(*b*) (i) Advantages:
Product endorsement helps to promote a good image for the organisation as people will associate the celebrity with the organisation. (1 mark)
If the celebrity is very well known and successful it can therefore help the organisation increase its sales. (1 mark)

Disadvantages:

It is an expensive method of promotion because celebrities charge large sums of money for their services. (1 mark)

The organisation must carefully ensure that it chooses the correct celebrity to promote the image of the product it wants to have otherwise it will not be as successful. (1 mark)

Any negative publicity the celebrity has had or could have in the future can have a negative impact upon the sales of the product. (1 mark)

Maximum of 2 marks for advantages and 2 marks for disadvantages.

(ii) The Advertising Standards Authority monitors advertising and other forms of promotion to ensure that organisations have created them to the standard expected. (1 mark)

Any complaints made by members of the public regarding adverts would be investigated by by the Advertising Standard Authority. (1 mark)

The Advertising Standard Authority has the ability to influence an organisation by insisting adverts and promotions are changed if they contain information that is wrong. (1 mark)

HINT The question asks for the reasons why it exists and the influence it can have. Your answer must address both of these points.

(c) Advantages:

An appraisal system aims to ensure employees are working to the best possible standard with the goal of achieving the aims of the organisation. (1 mark)

It allows for the strengths and the development needs of an employee to be identified and for the employee to receive feedback from their line manager on their performance at work. (1 mark)

Employees who are working extremely well have the opportunity to be identified for promotion and motivation can increase. (1 mark)

Disadvantages:

Employees receiving a negative appraisal can become demotivated and unproductive. (1 mark)

Time consuming for the organisation to administer and carry out. (1 mark)

Appraisals only work if the employee is willing to accept and act on the development needs and training given to them. (1 mark)

HINT It is not necessary to give a description of an appraisal because this is not asked for.

(d) (i) **Any 2 for 1 mark each:**

Careers Scotland, Business Gateway, Princes Trust, Banks/Lenders, Inland Revenue, Local Authorities, Local Enterprise Agencies.

(ii) **Any 3 for 1 mark each:**

Information on how to carry out market research.

Methods of recording financial information.

Information on finding business premises.

Information on choosing a suitable business name.

Information on recruiting and selecting new employees.

Information on putting together a business plan.